JOURNEY OF A BROKEN MAN

SIMON J MARTON

This book is for any man who has ever thought he was

a mistake...

The legal bit

Despite my intentions to create a book which is interesting, well-informed and sometimes amusing, it is not possible to please everyone. You are free to disagree with what I have written. You might even rip it up, burn it or simply give it to a charity shop. Burning books is a last resort though. It's hardly *Mein Kampf* or even *The Satanic Verses*. Recycling is superior.

To the best of my knowledge I have recollected my thoughts to express what I saw, and what I and others have been through, as true. There may be the odd part which a reader calls into question, concerning accuracy. I certainly don't write to mislead or cause offence.

My caveat here is that although I have written about others, protected identities as far as possible and researched to back up my findings, I am still fallible. I have tried to portray everything in a reasonable and balanced way. I hope this comes across.

Dedications

Dear reader, I thank you for buying this book. I really appreciate every copy sold.

With love to my beautiful wife, Helen and my family (Eli, Sacha, Faith and Noah) who probably know me and my various moods better than anyone. With thanks to friends like Gavin Mayall, Bobby C, Jason Whiley and Jammer Stanton for keeping me on my toes and keeping me going. Also, to my dad, Gino: he made me what I am today. An ageing man who likes chain-sawing trees and chasing squirrels on his days off. (Like father, like son.)

Thank you to all my contributors for your various stories esp. in Chapter Seven. My gratitude to men like Dr. Stu Farrimond, Magnus Christie, Kevin Cook and Stefan Cooke who encouraged me greatly to keep writing after they read my previous book. I appreciate the various radio interviews from established DJs like Nahil Arthanayake, Mandy Morrow, Rob Bayly, Leo Jones and Robbie Dixon.

Thank you to Ali Hull (*Sorted* magazine), Les R. (*Captain Jetson*), Ted Thornhill (*Daily Mail*), Harriet Mallinson (*The Express*), Kara Godfrey (*The Sun*) and Christopher Kai (*'Gifters'* podcast) for taking a chance on my story and thereby granting me global exposure. This has cemented my resolve to climb further and see just what lies up those mountains which others have fearlessly ascended.

With thanks to all those whom I have ever worked alongside, both on the ground and in the air for your good humour, camaraderie and professionalism.

The highest thank you continually goes to Jesus who has never let me go.

I am a proud supporter of R.N.I.D. (formerly 'Action on Hearing Loss') to raise awareness of how other musicians, motorcyclists and airline workers could prevent damage to their hearing through exposure to loud music and amplified instruments. (Tinnitus really does suck, but it was fun getting it.)

I also support several major supermarkets, usually on a weekly basis alongside my wife. Your trolleys and shelves are always neatly stacked, and your staff are usually a credit to you. You know who you are.

Recommendations

Visit www.mindcanyon.co.uk for services

Email info@mindcanyon.co.uk for general enquiries

What We Do

At Mindcanyon, we want everyone to understand their own mind, how it works and how to keep it healthy. We're here to help organisations, like yours, educate their employees on the importance of taking care of their own mental health, as well as each other's.

We can help you and your employees manage those minds. And what's in it for you, as an employer? Your team will be happier and healthier, which means they'll be more motivated and productive through our mental health, workplace well-being and suicide first aid training.

It's not just about mental health; it's about mental fitness.

Foreword

Dear Friend,

I was born in 1970, a good year I'm told, and I am (on paper) most of the way through my life. It's been a blast so far. It's also had some very low points, been a long slog and a test of endurance. One day I will breathe my last, thankful for the days I have been given and the experiences which I have endured and enjoyed. I'm a man who feels like a boy, one half 'Mr. Responsible' with bills that never diminish and the other half, my twenty-one-year-old carefree-self still in a band dreaming of making it. I wonder if it's still OK to wear my baseball cap back to front. I like chilled Prosecco from a flute, the odd pint of *Kronenbourg* with a dash of lime, lasagne with *Insalata Caprese*, 650 cc monster trailies, black drum kits and laughter. I'm still a simple man but no longer in his late forties, who has now realized that the idea of owning a wine cellar might be too small a dream and too achievable. There's far more to living than my small-mindedness. But I do like a nice Rioja, especially if it has one of those wire nets around it.

This is probably the book that I really wanted to write, before the idea mutated into '*Journey of a Reluctant Air Steward.*' I still don't feel like a 'proper' author. Admittedly, that book has done me some favours, opened new doors and has allowed me to continue writing and developing my style. This book has a very different flavour, as it concerns 'identity' which is something I began to explore but didn't fully expand upon, as anecdotes about the airline industry got in the way. You know what they say about male cabin crew? Yes, I know what you're thinking, but I bet you there are plenty who struggle with who they are, and not in obvious ways.

Over the years, I have felt inside that I don't quite measure up to what a man should be. When I look at the abilities of a lot of tradespersons or even friends who are good with car engines or who excel at DIY, that's when inadequacy starts to creep in. So, Helen bought me a *Stihl* chainsaw to compensate. (Now I can chop down trees with TPOs on them.) It started off with comparing my drumming abilities with a session drummer friend of mine and wanting to throw my sticks away. (He could play *everything* I could, whereas I could play about *that* much of what he can.) It's taken me literally decades to work out that there's enough room in the world for both of us. I'm still not as good as Uncle Rob, but I am louder.

As I write this foreword, I am balancing my laptop on the kids' trampoline outside in the garden. The world has been apparently usurped by a virus that has forced us all to stay at home to avoid cross-contamination where we all have to *'act like you've got it.'* Everyone looks at each other with a mis-trust, veiled by masked smiles, as if to say; *"Isn't this surreal? But keep your distance!"* I am fortunate enough to live in a quiet neighbourhood on the edge of rolling countryside, the warmth of the summer morning tempered by a slight chill in the air. The trees are starting to bud, and blossoms are full and white, a stark beauty against the deep blue skies. A flock of racing pigeons and doves in an arrowhead formation is soaring past every few minutes, their wings beating with flashes of platinum and grey, like an airborne shoal of silverfish. This feels like peace. A glimpse of heaven.

Just a few miles away in the city where I grew up, there is outward beauty, a rich veneer and a luxurious sheen which belies the darker underbelly. This is where the gargoyles of anxiety, depression, despondence and even despair guard their territorial rights, from high above and over those who have given into them. Within these pages, you'll read real-life stories of men who stumbled, fell and attempted to get themselves back up, with a little help. Getting to a place of full recovery, however, proved elusive, and most of these men fell prey to demons and lies that were so strongly convincing, that they were like helpless flies caught in a spider's web, unable to cut through the strands that held them captive, and became hopeless. Still, they cling onto life and its daily passage, but a few didn't make it out at all....

This isn't a book that will entertain you in the traditional sense, and it isn't in any way meant to sensationalize the normal. I am compelled to tell these stories as I feel that far too much is left in the shadows, taboo or simply untold. These are stories of everyday men like you and I, who through a series of unfortunate events, illnesses and choices, ended up in worse predicaments. I rubbed shoulders with many professionals in the Adult Social Care field, including GPs, mental health specialists, social workers, occupational therapists, pharmacists and many more. They could tell some equally dark tales I am sure.

If you're wondering why I chose to write about men, it's just that I feel compelled to write a book by a man for men. It's not that I don't like women, far from it. Women have some amazing stories to tell. I could have included so many, but the title wouldn't have worked that great, would it? I've got a great story about a lady who was a friend of another lady, a client of mine whom I was covering for a colleague. She asked me if I could get her a new replacement proper front door to her house as she had been promised one for two years. She showed me the fire door which was solid but industrial. It turned out she had grassed up a local drug dealer and in return he and his henchmen had thrown a petrol bomb through the letter box. She only just managed to escape with her two young children through the downstairs blaze. (Oh, and it took me just two days to sort her front door out with a repairs manager with a choice of three colours. Petrol blue was not one of the choices.)

Get yourself settled and prepare to be shaken a little if this knowledge is new to you, or if it seems a little too close to home. I write not as an expert, but more as a messenger; someone caught on the frontline, winging it as best as he could through situations that were thrown my way. Sometimes in my old role, I felt out of my depth, yet I still had to remain measured, helpful and resourceful, giving a ray of hope where I could, in the form of a practical lifeline. I really enjoyed a lot about my pathway at the time and getting a result for my clients was somewhat addictive – if you'll pardon the pun. A few years on and I understand that poor sense of identity and struggles with keeping your mental health stable apply to *anyone, including me.*

I do also privately wonder if sometimes we are a little too reverent about our approach to 'mental health' (MH). Yes, it is a serious subject but it's not all doom and gloom. People can still smile and even laugh occasionally. That includes my old clients as well as myself and others I have written about. Since those times I have tried other doors, some of which have remained closed to me, while others have opened wide to my delight. Maybe, just maybe, a life full of risk and courage will make us live like we ought to!

Talking of risk, I've just had a flashback to the day of my vasectomy. Helen was using the car, so I chose to cycle there. Midway through the short op at the surgery, the doctor looked up from between my legs and happily announced, "One down, one to go!" (*"You've used that line before",* I thought to myself.) On the way home, I treated myself to a pack of custard donuts and a box of paracetamol from Tesco Express and completed the rest of the two-mile journey home side-saddle in the rain. Man, I ached badly, but I felt a little lighter.

They say everyone has a story inside of them. (Some might say that I have too many and should give others a chance. I would, but I quite like my stories.) So, here are mine and my interpretations. I have split the book into two parts to reflect my varied experiences while at work, and my equally varied experiences in my own life, but sometimes there's a crossover. One day, we might even share a bottle of Syrah, who knows? With the world as it's heading, I fear a crisis of MH is imminent. I hope these chapters might awaken something inside you. You're not alone. These stories may make you go quiet. Always watch the quiet ones.

Simon J Marton

Spring 2021

A prelude

Picture a young boy aged maybe six or seven sat alongside others older than him, in a school classroom sometime in the mid-seventies. He's a smiley young man, finding his feet in the world. His folks work hard at their catering business down the street and want him to have the best start they can afford, so they send him and his sister to this tiny privately-run school which has no more than about 12 pupils. He has a fear. He is often called to recite his 'two-times table' from his little desk in that dark classroom two floors up. His teacher listens as he can't ever quite make it past 'six'. He stumbles at the 'four times two' stage and is in trepidation as he knows what's coming. His teacher orders him out to stand in front of the class. His lips start to quiver as she towers over him with her voice raised in a harsh Irish-Catholic tone:

"You lazy wicked boy! Why haven't you learnt your tables properly?! Stand there in front of everyone. Hold your hand out!"

The young boy trembles as his body braces for the shock of a wooden metre rule to slap forcefully across his hand. As the pain hits, he cannot hold back the tears and loses control of his bladder, a steady trickle flowing from his shorts down his leg. A puddle forms at his feet as the dumpy woman berates him again.

"Look at what you've done!"

Other children before him are stifling their laughter. He continues to cry looking downwards, wishing he could be away from here. Shamed in front of everyone, another teacher, younger and kinder takes him away to be cleaned up. This happens on several occasions, yet his parents never seem to do anything about it. Either they never know the full picture or are too busy working. The thought even crosses his mind that they do know.

Years later, the young man aged maybe thirteen walks through town with his dad, when his father stops to say 'hello' to an old but familiar lady outside a bus shelter. His dad is friendly towards her as is his way and introduces his tall son to the lady who is now considerably shorter than the young man remembers. She looks up semi-smiling through her bifocals, but the young man barely says a word beyond 'Hello'. She knows and he knows. Strangely, his father doesn't, and probably would downplay what his son might describe.

Over four decades later, he vividly remembers those moments of shame, the laughter and the pool of urine. Those moments have followed him like chasing shadows or like the sounds of children taunting their victim at primary school, surrounding him in a circle, singing their cruel song until the child breaks. His wound is that somewhere deep inside, he still feels like that little boy....

Contents

Part One

Part Two

PART ONE

Chapter One

When one door closes...

Risk is one thing and reality another. We men need to pay the bills and keep the ship running so it's not always easy to take a risk. Just like the committal to the children's death slide, over the edge and the dreaded fearful moment of truth: the release and drop down the vertical wall. Whenever I've been poised for the jump, my heart has hovered in my mouth as I confront the fear of failure, yet taking risks makes all men come alive.

Into the valley...

My time in the airline industry had spanned 16 years on and off. On my very first day I was in the flight deck for an aborted landing into Faro, and for my last flight, I was again sat in the flight deck as we carried just one passenger from Manchester to London. I had finished working up at Heathrow Airport (LHR) serving others at 39,000ft and had returned home to the West Country. That old door I ensured was now in manual mode, pin secured and firmly locked. I was done permanently with airlines, and it was time to come home to my family and find work locally. One door closes and yet so many more still seem closed. It was obvious for me that I should keep an open mind. The very real risk was not finding that work. Early years music-teaching, ad hoc support-work and cycling instructing were openings I found along the way, but I ended up working for a housing association quite by accident. I had been working on some neighbourhood mediation cases in the next city, and a couple of them had been for a housing provider which I knew very little about. I made enquiries, hoping to score some extra mediation work and instead found a couple of potential jobs centering around the Older persons service, 'sheltered housing schemes' and 'care and support'. Having applied and having been screened, I got through both selection stages and was duly offered the role of support worker/ officer. Permanent employment at last after nearly two years of bits and pieces. Just don't look at my CV; it's all over the place.

I mentioned mediation just now. A mediator's role is to stand between parties impartially to draw them to a peaceful agreement moving forward. In other words, *conflict resolution*. These cases I was involved in were between neighbours who had often started out as friendly, but over time had become adversaries. The root causes of the mistrust could be as simple as excessive noise, boundary disagreements, loss of parking spaces, cultural differences or even simple misunderstandings. The most extreme case I saw involved two families living next door to each other in a notorious suburb. The male heads had fallen foul of each other, causing the most needlessly aggressive intentions towards their opposites. It was very difficult to remain impartial when faced with a mother and her three young boys on a sofa; an infant, a four-year old and a nine-year old all eating ice creams at 8.30pm when they should have been in bed. Instead they were listening to their father ranting about their neighbours with vicious and destructive threats through the weed-filled atmosphere. Dad also growled the following; *"I hate my mother for what she did to me. If I ever saw her again, I'd slit her throat. But I hate my neighbour more."* (At that point, my hand instinctively went to cover my own throat.) A few weeks later, myself and a fellow mediator would start the low-key resolution process at a neutral venue (a locally hired room) with the two mothers present as a start. Although it was a difficult atmosphere, at least these two were prepared to talk. After twenty minutes into the session, one of them broke down in tears to admit that the last year of this tension had taken such a toll on her eldest boy, that she had discovered him only just in time trying to hang himself in his bedroom. It showed me that children absorb more than we think.

My first week at my new job was fairly corporate and office-based, getting to know the systems and procedures. They gave me a mug, a pen and a basic *Nokia*. A year or two down the line, I would be given a *Samsung* tablet, which would speed up an awful lot of applications, research enquiries and allow me unbridled access to *YouTube*. I had a couple of low-key visits to high-end retirement living flats as well as to a couple of elderly residents out in more rural settings. I shadowed a few colleagues and was briefed in the front of the car pre-visits about anything I should know. We were dealing with very vulnerable people, and I wasn't fully prepared for battle. Into the valley I wandered. Little did I know what was awaiting me.

Diamond Geezers

The funding of the whole service was largely down to the local authority's Adult Social Care and Support budget, where work was subbed out to the chosen bidders. Levels of support were banded into tiers of time named after precious stones. For example, the highest level was worth up to two hours of support time/ week which included travel time, logging outcomes, phone calls as well as the actual face-to-face time spent with a client. The next banding down was a little less work, but up to one and a quarter hours of input/ support per week. Medium/ low input bands were less involved, but you could find yourself absorbed by a particular problem once in a while which would far exceed the allotted time, such as an impromptu hospital visit or an accident.... Basic-plan customers simply had an emergency services lifeline alarm only and a yearly review check to see if anything had changed. The careline 24/7 alarm system was common to all customers as a basic necessity, supplied with a pendant trigger worn on the body and was worth its weight in gold (pun intended).

In order to maintain the levels of funding for the service, all officers were required to demonstrate 'outcomes' on a spreadsheet. For example, if you felt that on a visit you had managed to *'prevent a client from being admitted to hospital'* by your intervention, that was an outcome code you could claim. This would save the NHS the cost of a bed and associated care, worth about £3000/ week. In the middle, there might be outcomes such as *'help customer to achieve paid employment'* or *'refer client to specialist drugs & alcohol service'*. At the other end of the scale it could have been something so simple as a chat during a visit which would directly *'reduce social isolation'*. Another tick on the spreadsheet and confirmation that the service was justified. There was an awful lot of last-minute keyboard-tabbing to do as the deadline for outcomes loomed every quarter and the boss breathed down our necks. One of the desirable aspects of the person specification was 'experience in inter-agency working'. This basically meant working alongside social services (Adult Social Care), GPs and hospital-personnel, charitable organisations and occasionally the police... By the time would I leave my job nearly four years later, I would have accumulated so much inter-agency experience that my confidence zoomed through the roof in dealing with the many involved and harrowing circumstances that I would be a party to. It's a wonder I didn't end up with PTSD myself. The team was a dispersed collective of about a dozen workers, all equipped with a personal safety device – an emergency call alarm disguised as an I.D. badge. Ingenious. The only thing you had to do was remember to discreetly hold the button down ahead of calling into someone's home and speak out time, address and expected duration of stay. This would be recorded on the call-centre system so that if you triggered the alarm in a threatening situation, the conversation could be listened into and police-help summoned to that address. There were thankfully more mis-triggers of the alarm than real-life dangerous predicaments, but it didn't stop you feeling like *Bodie and Doyle* or even a pretend *Jason Bourne* as you spoke into the contraption before and after every visit.

Once I had inherited my own list of clients, I could make my mark on the role. If truth be told, even though I had briefly done some brain-injury client-support work in the past, I was now left to my own wits and savvy to engage with customers and work out ways forward with them. The little old ladies who just enjoyed a chat about what was going on in the news, being taken shopping locally or organising their garden recycling were easy-enough clients, but I craved working with the more-complicated males who always had more interesting issues going on, that I could get my teeth into. I wasn't to be disappointed.

Chapter Two

Housing, benefits and 'the system'

I can't go into this story without giving you some background information. Social housing and state benefits often go hand-in-hand. When you need state help, you need it. (I was to see how the two are often intertwined and how many people were caught in a 'benefits-trap', where it might become easier and sometimes even advantageous not to work, but to claim benefit payments.) That said, none of my clients could have ever returned to work, on account of either their physical health or their mental health, often both. You will also see how benefits payments are not automatic....

Social housing

If you've come across the term, but haven't really understood the concept, it's fairly straightforward. It's housing that is sometimes referred to as 'council-housing', which is a little misleading as it is often provided by non-council organisations (registered housing providers {RPs} and housing associations {HAs}) and is subsidised for those who cannot, for whatever reason, afford regular rental (market) property prices. A social landlord can be a council or an RP. It comes in at a 'social rent' (aka 'formula rent') which is calculated using a formula based on property value, size, average income for the region plus 5%, and is always lower than 'affordable rent'. It can get confusing when it is mislabeled as 'affordable rent' which is actually a little higher in cost. Social rent is usually 80% of market rent rate. And still people interchange the terms, mainly professionals.

To be eligible you could be vulnerable in any number of ways, including being a single parent family, elderly, disabled or simply unemployed or homeless through circumstances. It is possible in social housing to apply to purchase your house or flat subject to one of two routes: 'right to buy' (council property) or 'right to acquire' (housing association). Once you buy, you are responsible outright for your home and upkeep. None of my clients ever had the means or the desire to do this.

Moving home: bidding and 'local connection'

You have to register to be on a long waiting list that is on the council's home-availability database where you 'bid' for your preferred home, usually in the knowledge that there could be up to several hundred people all bidding for the same property. The more you bid, even if it is strategically by clicking on a home you have no chance of being in the running for, the better your profile becomes as an active home-seeker. Everyone starts off on the same level or banding, but what really does increase your chances is demonstrating an evidenced medical need to push you up a band. You will usually have to prove something called 'a local connection' which is as it sounds; evidence that the area you want to live in has some family-tie or work location. Even if you are 'successful' in achieving a viewing, you might be viewing that flat or that house with 10 to 20 others who have made the shortlist. The lettings agent will make a note of any no-shows or anyone he thinks may not be suitable for financial or concerning issues. He or she will whittle the shortlist down eventually to maybe three or four potential tenants who might be existing housing tenants of the same RP.

An offer will be made to the top-of-the-list applicant who either accepts or turns down the property, and it then passes down the list to the second and then the third. RPs and HAs are keen that a property should not be 'void' for long. If it can be turned around within a couple of weeks, ready for the next occupier, this is good business and ensures the chain of rental income is kept as intact as possible. Much like the private rental market, an empty property is wasting capital and revenue simultaneously, so the quicker it can be earning rent, the better. In moves the new tenant (or tenants), and the flow continues. It is well-known that moving-house is one of the most stressful situations we come across in our lives. That, relationship breakdown, job loss and bereavement. (For a pilot, it's the take-off and landing phases. Sorry, I had to get an airline analogy in somewhere...)

What must it be like for those who suffer some, or even all of these situations in a very short time?

A simple overview of Benefits

Housing Benefit (HB) is the local authority's contribution to your rent (private or otherwise) and is worked out according to what your regular income is. It is set to a maximum and is called a Local Housing Allowance set to each property type. Council Tax Benefit is a relief of part or full on Council Tax (CT), and is covered by the local authority again. Failure to pay CT is classed as a criminal offence, so it is wise to keep this as a 'priority debt.' I have heard stories of old people actually being convicted of this offence and spending a short time in jail. The newspapers loved to report this injustice. It sold a few more copies and kept conversations going between strangers at bus stops.

At the time I was in my advocacy role, a benefit which was being phased in, but is now fully established (yes, another flying expression for you) is *Universal Credit (UC)*. In simple terms, it is all someone's benefits payments wrapped into one, to include housing-related as well as health-related ones. (A new application for UC can still take about six weeks before the applicant sees any money at all, leaving them to beg, borrow or even steal in the meantime.) The downside we were aware of was that it would now give full autonomy to the payee to budget and take ownership of all the payments, when previously, housing benefit for example, was taken at source to pay the rent directly to the housing provider or the private landlord. Dangerous ground for landlords to see their tenants suddenly in a great position of credit where some had never handled their own rent payments before. A certain amount of 'education' was needed for those who were new to this and were in danger of 'mishandling' their income.

The main benefits I dealt with included the following:

Jobseekers Allowance (JSA) and Employment Seekers Allowance (ESA) for those of employable ages. Those paper forms could go on to about 30 pages or more.

PIP (Personal Independence Payment) took over from DLA (Disability Living Allowance which had 2 parts; mobility and daily living.) This was a benefit that could be worth up to £320 per month and had to be filled in correctly with as much supporting evidence as possible from the medical profession.

Severe Disability Premium was an add-on to DLA, that could be claimed by the applicant. Its name was entirely misleading and that's all I'll say.

Attendance Allowance was an extra benefit that could be worth an average of £80/week for those who could demonstrate they needed extra care help or were unable to look after themselves entirely without paid intervention or unpaid family help. It could take about three to four hours to properly fill in the AA form I found, and that was me going like *Speedy Gonzalez*. It would be pointless filling it in by describing the applicant as a capable brave soldier, for you had to show what a really bad day involved, such as precarious nightly toilet-visits, reliance on help with personal care or inability to cook a meal unless aided, to be in with a chance of scoring success.

I was to see a direct link between the financial benefits, DWP (Department for Work and Pensions), alcohol, drugs, depression, acute anxiety, co-morbidity (two illnesses at same time), aggression, paranoia, agoraphobia, and the medications for depression, mainly *Sertraline, Temazepam* and *Diazepam*. The side-effects for those were astonishing: nausea, drowsiness and disturbing dreams were common.

Death sentence

In my few years working in the sector on the frontline, I saw how benefits are the financial lifeline to so many who simply are unable through mental health conditions especially, to hold down any form of employment. Anxiety and depression are so widespread, even for those of us with jobs, that you might understand how a simple (online) job application and even the thought of contemplating an interview would be enough to completely drive a person with underlying anxiety into sheer panic. These everyday undertakings might as well be mountains covered in ice; completely unscalable and the end of the known world. It's the same with money and when its supply is blocked. I once made a phone-call relating to a stopped-benefits payment on behalf of a client belonging to a colleague whom I was covering for, and she completely came to pieces, shouting behind me as I tried to maintain a professional tone; *"I need that money! I need that money!"* Of course, the call-handler could hear the commotion. This type of call was frequent for me, and so were the interjections my clients would make, as if interrupting and background hysteria was going to make the agent more pliable. I'd just do my best to keep a moderate tone, clinging onto facts rather than emotions.

It is quite normal for people on benefits to undergo an official periodic review of their circumstances, in much the same way as an employee does with their manager. However, there is one crucial difference; for those on benefits for a mental and even physical disability, the receipt of a letter inviting them for an assessment can lead them into weeks of extra anxiety, on top of what they already endure, with the extreme worry that 'the system' is out to rob them of the little they have been entitled to. These brown envelopes (in common with so many brown envelopes you receive in the post) signaled fear and finality. For many of my charges, they may as well have been a death sentence. I would have to work harder with coming up with a plan to discuss all the possible outcomes, including the worst and how we might deal with that. More on this later....

The assessment appointment: setting you up to fail?

I was to discover quite by accident through a phone conversation with a doctor's secretary, that the assessments were geared to setting people up for failure in some subversive ways. She cited the following (paraphrased):

"Many DWP appointments that I have seen are booked for around 9 a.m. with their partner-assessors. This means that someone will have had to wake up extra early (which is difficult if you're on medication) to organize an expensive taxi which they can't really afford, to take them to the bus station to wait for a connecting bus to (the city), where they may have to walk to the assessment centre. Whether or not they arrive alone or aided, the cameras will be set up in the car park and/or the entrance as well as in the waiting room to observe how they act. They are watched the whole time to see if they are as bad as they claim to be basically. If they make it to the centre on time, they will have proven they have the ability to organize themselves to get to an appointment by journeying through rush hour; the busiest and most stressful time of the day. By doing this unaided, they will have done themselves no favours as this will be taken by the examiners that they are not as bad as they make out, and all because they have probably worried themselves to death about making it through for this vital appointment...."

That alone was an eye-opener for me. I was to find out other things about the assessments which made me deeply dubious about the whole affair. *Was the whole thing rigged to weed out the less-honest, or was it geared to set everyone up for a fail?*

For these reasons alone, I would try my best to book home-visit assessments for my clients. Now, the health-assessing agencies contracted by the DWP to carry out these tests didn't like to advertise this option, but they were perfectly normal and routine. I preferred them, not just for the GPs secretary's observations above, but because it allowed the medical assessor to observe my clients in their natural habitat as it were. I sat in on a handful where possible to support my clients where my quiet presence would help to quell their nervousness. Occasionally I might intervene to clarify a response to the examining medical professional, explaining the position with perhaps a more lucid answer than my client's.

Panicked into compliance

Other customers would be panicked by the letters into feeling the compulsion to go, lest their whole benefits claim would be annulled, and they would be left with no income. This was a very real fear. I would have to argue harder for the reasoning *not* to go in these situations, because their whole claim might be unraveled; see the GP's secretary's statements above. Here's why...

One retired gentleman ignored all my advice and my work with the assessor-agency to organise a home visit, because he felt that attending the assessment was 'the right thing to do' by obeying the letter. So, he did. He managed to get there on time, across two cities through rush hour with no assistance. When I asked him why he did it, he apologised but it wasn't his 'sorry' I was after. I just hoped he hadn't sabotaged himself. Ten days later, he phoned me in a complete panic, with a letter in hand. His benefits had suddenly been stopped, with nothing in his bank account. (They had assessed him at the centre and thus decided he was capable after all.) There was nothing I could do as I was leaving that employment and it would have to be handed over to another colleague, causing uncertainty, anguish and delay to any future income. That's what you get for doing the right thing. One of my clients even thought that because I worked for an organisation that held 'power' over him, I was part of 'the system'. Truth is that we are all a part of 'the system', all gripped by its invisible hand. Comply or suffer the consequences.

Wasted days

Every Monday afternoon, I would visit a beautiful block of flats to visit *T*, a retired gentleman who was on medication for anxiety, that would see him sleep through the day until about 3pm, then awaken for the evenings, which would be absorbed by nostalgia TV and his own thoughts. There was always a musty smell in his flat, as though it needed a good airing for a week just to get back to zero and start again with a neutral odour. His décor was the basic housing association magnolia, punctuated with old charity shop pictures of a Hawaiian beauty, an art deco flat with a spiky plant in the foreground and a framed print of a little girl crying. Those prints of children crying always disturbed me. His furniture and TV were ageing but usable. (That same block of flats had leaseholders who had parted with a couple of hundred thousand pounds each for their flats, whilst in the same block, roughly 30% of tenants would be on housing benefit paying a social rent.)

T had been a tradesman who had worked in a couple of European countries as well as England and had retired early owing to alcohol intake. He had been forced to leave his old flat because of 'a situation', which was very hazy. It sounded like an eviction, with the added sadness of seeing most of his usable household belongings cleared and thrown out by a commercial firm. He had been moved to this new flat a year or two earlier, where he had started to rebuild his life, but he was becoming laden with debts once more. He had been handed to me by another colleague who had probably taken him as far as she could without crumbling in sheer frustration. Week by week we would cover the same old ground, which was usually a discussion of what he had been up to, as he rubbed the sleep from his eyes, and a utility bill or a letter from the DWP in a brown envelope passed over to me for my perusal. He had 'ways' to make small savings by cheating the system such as removing wiring from certain parts of the boiler, so he could avoid a standing charge for heating usage for the whole building. Even then, he managed to build up large arrears simply because he didn't think it was fair that he should pay utility bills as a pensioner.

He was consumed by fixations on money, how the pensions services in the UK and abroad had robbed him of what was rightfully his, and how I didn't understand 'the system' as I was apparently a part of it. I used to explain to him that I was just as much under 'the system' as he was, but his mistrust was so deeply rooted that it was unshakeable in its delusion. Quoting a handful of personal stories, he would tell me how government workers and those who are in charge of taxes, pensions and benefits were *'trained to lie, conceal and force the public into hardship, unless they were confronted at their own game.'* (Looking back, there was an element of truth here.) He would turn on me quite often, as if I was in on it all, apologising occasionally as if he started to comprehend, but he was a prisoner of his own beliefs and misgivings. Being an alcoholic by his own admission and using this as justification for extra benefits payments, he still liked beer, or 'a bevvy or two' as he described it. Whenever I asked him to explain the benefits he was on, his heckles were up and he would become defensive and semi aggressive, telling me I didn't understand, and how he was entitled to that money.

All around him was a network of drinkers who would frequent the pub at the cinema complex in town, and smoke in lines outside the doors. From that network, I would be told of the odd person who had died every now and then; another 'someone' who didn't make it. Sometimes the remnants of belongings which were left behind would be distributed to people like *T* if they lived in the same block. It saved housing voids staff the extra work of clearing heavy items down several flights of stairs if they could be claimed by others instead. Those items would serve as reminders of the ones who had departed prematurely through their love of the strong stuff. The 'perks' of a tenant living across the way.

Week by week, I would use the 45 minutes to make calls on his behalf, urging him not to interrupt me, as I organised payment plans to avoid bailiff-action, ways forward with UK and European pension agencies to secure 'lost' payments and even cessation of a funeral plan contract which he had entered too quickly and then reconsidered. It took me several months' of intervention via personal calls, emails and *legalaise* letters to get two overpayment claims by the DWP of four figures each to be quashed. My way of working was to use fact, evidence and a personable approach to secure results like these, just like a 'real' lawyer might.

Here was a man who was on strong medication which would erase most of his days, unless there was a daytime appointment he had to make. Surfacing most afternoons, his breakfast was usually a defrosted cheesecake. I worked hard to get him onto a weekly bicycle-maintenance course at a local charity which he almost blew out. He would sometimes tell me of church-groups he might go to during the weekday evenings or at weekends, sometimes hooking up with people who could give him a lift across town and having meals together; it was obvious he was quite sociable. Some of his stories of days gone past were quite entertaining, even if they did involve quasi-dangerous mistakes on the job because he had had one too many beers at lunchtime. He used to snigger, revealing the gaps in his mouth where the decades of sugar-intake had taken some of his teeth away. For the main part though, I sensed *T*'s loneliness and fear of both the present and of the future, as though he was acutely aware of his life-clock ticking to an inexorable alarm. I don't know if he is still with us.

What had a man done to himself that would make him waste his days like this?

A 'severe' disability comes at a premium

It was usual for me to dart from one 'disaster' to another. I remember the morning well, when I went to see a family friend who lived close by. He was dying of cancer and had just a day or two of seeing another sunrise, so I went in to say my 'final goodbye', while his two young boys were at school, and as his wife sat on the nearby sofa. As I climbed back into the car, I could see I had five missed calls on my work mobile. It was *H*. It was very unusual for him to ring, so something must surely have been up. Excitedly, he answered the phone and exclaimed how he had been trying frantically to call me. This was the conversation:

"Simon, do you remember when I had that benefits form to fill in, and you told me you weren't going to touch it, and you sent me to CAB? *" (*Citizens Advice Bureau.)

I did. I had told him that as intelligent as I could be, there was no way I was going to touch that form as the slightest mistake could cost him his income, whereas Citizens Advice Bureau had the 'descriptors' which were the exact responses that the DWP were looking for to achieve the benefit. I had forced him to go with an urgency that day.

"Well, I just want to thank you for pushing me to go there. While filling in the form at CAB, they saw that there was an extra disability payment I should have been receiving; 'Severe Disability Premium'. I have just had a letter from the DWP; *they have backdated my claim two years and have put £8000 into my bank account this morning!* I can't believe it. Thank you for making me go there!"

I was thrilled for him as this was to be the biggest financial result I had ever been a part of securing, although it wasn't really myself who could take the credit. At the same time, I had just left the house of a dear man who would not see his family or anyone else again after the weekend. Meanwhile, this vulnerable client of mine was a retired single man who abused his body daily on alternate weeks. Even though, he said he would ring fence the money in an ISA to stop him spending it on drink, I struggled to reconcile the differences between these two men. I had compassion for both.

How hard it often is, to see each man as an individual with different needs and choices, and harder still to remain unbiased in the face of inequality?

I fought the law: an appeal for sense

I worked briefly with another client, *H*, who had been denied disability benefits despite being clearly an open and shut case. His cancer nurse and his GP couldn't believe that he had failed the application on two counts for a vital benefit payment of DLA. He also told me that one day in town a few months earlier, he had collapsed in the street through dizziness brought on by his condition. As he laid on the ground, he recalled most people walking on by, some laughing at him calling him a drunk, most ignoring his pain, but it was a schoolgirl who was the only one to show empathy. She had helped to pull him up back onto his feet. The Lettings Colleague told me he had recommended me as a good fit to work with *H*. I got in touch and set to work straight away. His flat was spotless and well-ordered, one of the few homes in which I would accept a cup of tea. He was quiet, polite and had that something we call a 'hard work ethic'; he was just out of work now while ill.

Approaching it with my legal head, I composed a letter of advocacy to the tribunals court, and with an air of authority told him that we were going down the appeal route and should "expect such and such to happen with a particular time framework of about three to four months". In truth I was operating on educated guesswork based upon my studies of *civil dispute resolution*, but I was convinced that my line of arguments would work. I picked apart the two points he had failed on and counteracted them with strong persuasive evidence. He allowed me to do what I thought was best and we waited. The story was to have a happy ending a few months later.

No more would his father have to drive a seventy-mile round-trip to help him go shopping, and he would at last have a couple of hundred extra pounds going into his account monthly to contribute towards daily living. The official government department headed letter informed *H*: '*The applicant's appeal has been allowed, the former decision of The Secretary of State has been overturned*', and a back-payment figure of over two thousand pounds had been paid into his account to cover the last year's payments which should have been. I had to stifle my tears over the phone when *H* told me that it was the first time that he had been able to buy new clothes in about two years. My work was complete. Unlike the song, I fought the law, but the law had not won.

How many times has the benefits system failed those who really need it? How many more men like H are out there, really needing this state help, and not getting it?

Other clients who asked me to take on the system included men whose partners were under a local authority Court of Protection order. My clients were adamant that it had been underhand and that their former partners either wanted to be with them, or somehow their finances had been incorrectly frozen. It would get to the point that I couldn't even talk to social workers as there were protocols and barriers in the way. On these occasions my hands were tied and acting any further on their behalf would become an impossibility. I would have to bow out politely. I had been told on my legal course that if you find yourself in a position where you can no longer act for a client because he/she has either an impossible case or has acted illegally, you simply state to the judge: 'I cannot continue to act, for professional reasons." (Judgey will get it apparently.)

Social housing doesn't mean a life of blank walls and hopelessness. These are people's homes, people with aspirations and abilities, not just disabilities. Homes where families are brought up, extended families are made and whole lifetimes are experienced. These homes have seen parties, laughter, tears of course, and triumphs along the way. For some of the men I knew, those homes were bases for more unsavoury activities....

Chapter Three

An imitation of life

Addictions come in many forms, but they all take away a man's self-worth and dignity. The short-term pleasure comes at a long-term cost....

High-rise help

In a sixties-built high-rise building slightly out of town, I was introduced to *D*, my new client who lived three floors up. The smell on entry into his flat was so overpowering that it nearly made me vomit, so I quickly learnt to hold my breath every time. Black mould was present in his flat, worst of all in the bathroom, and a choking smell of chlorine often overwhelmed me when I went to visit him in his natural habitat. I earmarked the poor hygiene, dirt, empties, kitchen, and makeshift net curtain holders (drawing pins), and his embarrassment at the way he lived. He suffered from obesity and was ashamed of his environment. He was an amiable enough fellow, yet his quick temper was usually bubbling below the surface...

Surprisingly, he would express a deep interest church and in God, and often asked me if I believed. We had the most interesting discussions about who God might be and the afterlife. His daily religion was not so pure, and there was the dichotomy; I would sometimes encounter him with his younger drinking buddies, and he told me frankly over the noise of the TV, that he didn't really enjoy drinking the cheap Chardonnays that were always opened in the mornings. (In flippant mood, I only just managed to stop myself recommending the slightly dearer *Italian Soave Classico* with its dry richness instead but thought better of it.) His cupboards were full of empties, and he was visibly embarrassed by the sight of all those wine bottles, two-litre plastic cider containers and lager cans that had built up over the months. I removed 6 black bin liners of bottles and disposed of them at the tip. He wanted salvation, but he couldn't quite see past the present and into the future. Small flies continued to hover over the wine glasses.

This 'support' carried on for about 18 months and I was often at a loss as to how I might actually be helping *D* in any way at all, bar reporting repairs for his flat, sorting out and updating government pensions claims and re-organising GP appointments. At his request, we also got contract cleaners in at his cost, to really hammer the living conditions into something resembling habitable.

When he was finally called into the local hospital, it would turn out to be his last trip from his flat. He died within four days, as his liver finally gave way, to a lifestyle of constant heavy drinking from seemingly innocent cheap white wine. When I went to gain access to his flat for the *NTQ (Notice to Quit),* I glanced around at the table where a pile of letters, some keys and a handful of personal effects lay. It saddened me to think that he never would have thought it would be the last time he would see his home. When I met his sister and his brother-in-law, they were so well-adjusted that the contrast was acute. She revealed her deceased brother's gambling habit and an inability to look after money, that often resulted in his anger and his motives being fully revealed. It had resulted in them being estranged for a long while, as he was too volatile to be around. She said something I won't forget. She and her husband were next to his hospital bed, waiting for him to wake up, and as he did so, she told me his face looked innocent and childlike, reminding her of when they used to play as children, brother and sister. Now he was vulnerable and softly spoken, and not the nasty, self-centred man he had become in adulthood.

His funeral day arrived, and as I entered, I saw there was a surprisingly large number of attendees there for such an isolated figure. It was down to me to liaise with the vicar for direction on the service, and although it was an unconventional start to a funeral, the welcome music was the theme to ITV's *'This Morning'*, chosen only because that was what he would usually have blaring from the TV on my weekly visits. I got up to speak, where no-one else dared and it centred on judgement and how it would be too easy to look at him and judge him, after all Jesus didn't come for the ones who think of themselves as sorted, but the ones like D. (I could see the men literally itching to get to the pub.)

No more procrastinating, no more cheap wine, no more mould and bleach. The end of a life spent pursuing an imitation of life.

The Addicted Film Star

It was a cold April day when Guy and I rang the front doorbell, then entered the door next to the tattoo parlour and climbed the four flights of stairs to get to his top floor apartment. Guy knocked on the private door to his own staircase, calling to let him know we were there, and he answered to come on up. I glanced towards a dirty kitchenette and a semi-obscured bathroom, before entering the small living room. Settled into a battered and threadbare armchair, huddling next to a barely working radiator was my client-to-be. My first encounter with *P* was an uneasy one. The curtain-less windows rattled in the wind, revealing the grey drizzled skies outside, and as Guy and I found a couple of stools to perch upon, I looked around the room to take in *P*'s living quarters.

The first thing that caught my eye was his soiled duvet and mattress laid straight on the floor to the right of his chair. It looked as warm and inviting a bed, as a coil of rusty barbed wire. Loose papers, brown envelopes, ashtrays, an old radio tuned into Radio 4 and a couple of small empty whiskey bottles gave me the clues. He was old, tired and resigned to life as it was. He had immense problems climbing the stairs to get to his flat, and this would have been enough of a surface reason to get him moved. A move had been tried before, but I was to discover that *P* was a dark horse. When I looked at him, his face reminded me instantly of the actors who would play Roman Centurions in fifties Hollywood films: he had a Roman nose. He was also playing a darker role, with no Elizabeth Taylor in sight.

Guy had also let me into one fact- P would frequently 'go under the radar' and this was quite normal. I remember seeing him by accident from across the street and I watched him as I made a call to him, only to see the phone being looked at and slotted back into his pocket. It could be weeks sometimes that you wouldn't hear anything, despite trying. I remember one chilly autumnal day, waiting with my manager outside the main street door, considering breaking it down as an option if the spare keys didn't arrive. To all our understanding he could have been dead for weeks. It would be the local store-persons that were my eyes on the ground who would confirm he was still dropping in most mornings for his whiskey, so that was to be my only assurance that he was alive.

He also explained what exactly 'street methadone' was: basically, a user gets his prescription, drinks it in front of the chemist but doesn't actually swallow it. Instead he leaves with the liquid still in his mouth and spits it out into a container once outside and can sell the contents for £10/ time. P was a regular consumer of street methadone although he swore he was off it. I got to know that it was pointless trusting him, as he would only ever tell you what he thought you needed to hear. That was a common thread to many of my clients.

He would over time, as I got to know him, show me old photos of happier days with a smiling woman and his dark curly mop of hair, which disguised the fact that they were both cocaine, heroin and speed addicts. He also had recent letters with photos of his young niece and her boyfriend holding a baby, inviting him to visit them. I would urge him to take the coach to London, to break away and force himself, even if only for the day and a different view. He wouldn't even consider it.

I found him a new flat, but at each turn I was thwarted. Well, he thwarted himself really. If anyone was shifty, it was P that day. I watched him carefully as he acknowledged equally shifty people he knew in the forecourt, and he kept fumbling in his coat pocket for what could only have been a bottle or a packet. The lady from Lettings wasn't stupid and I am sure clocked everything. It was a complete *Catch 22* situation; because he had been a known-user, he wasn't fully trusted to keep other drug-users away from his home, he didn't look after his present home properly, and although he desperately needed ground floor accommodation because of his COPD (a medical condition- struggling with breathing) even the GPs strongly-worded letter to Lettings could not shift the fact that while he persisted in all the above, he was prevented from moving.

In an attempt to help him get out of his depressing living quarters and experience some fresh air, one summer's day I arranged to pick him up on the street corner. I watched him walk across the road, his svelte figure dressed in a black leather jacket, sporting a pair of dark framed Ray-bans. It was because of this that I called him 'film star'. If you were to put him in a genre though, I would suggest the style of *'Taxi Driver'*. We only drove about ten or fifteen minutes out of town and into the countryside where we chatted in a layby. Blue skies, green meadows and hills lined with oaks, birches and conifers. It was so simple, yet it was like an oasis.

One day I received a succession of panic calls from 'a friend' who told me "P was in a really bad way and it was a shocking failure" (less-politely said) "that no-one cared or was helping…". He had soiled himself multiple times and was so weak that he was taken to hospital. I traced him to his new bed and discussed things with his mental health nurse who advised me on what would need to change. They were truly on top of things at the hospital. He was not to move back to his flat but was nursed back to health in a specialist ward and moved to a care-home the other end of England. Quite by accident, I called him on the day he was enroute there in specialist transport. No-one thought I should be kept in the loop apparently. I privately hoped that he would end his days there, happier and free of temptations.

Many months later, he would end up back in the city, and back in his familiar haunts within questionable company. I could not endorse a housing application knowing he would certainly go back to his old ways. He did end up moving back, but this time I was not involved in any care/ support. His lady friend blamed me voraciously for not having terminated the previous tenancy properly and according to her, I was to be held personally liable for the £3,000 bill in back-rent now owed to the housing provider. The value of an email trail: I had done things by the book but hauled-up just so two managers could feel better about accusing me themselves. It wasn't the first time I had experienced a culture of blame. I left them to it, to continue the argument themselves as they seemed to be good at blaming there.

And what of our film star? He died within a few months, a colleague from Lettings later informed me, back to old habits. A tragic waste of life in glorious technicolor.

These two men died in squalor and had abused their bodies for most of their lives. Was there more that I could have done? What were they trying so hard to blank out? Was the truth of who they were so deeply troubling that they could not bear to face themselves?

A balancing act

K was a genuine chap, a similar age to me who obviously wanted to better himself, but he was a prisoner, both mentally and physically. He spoke quite openly to me on the open landing outside his flat on our first meeting as client/customer, following my initial introduction by my manager. (My manager had been dismissive of him, calling him 'just a p***head' in his handover to me.) I felt it was to be my calling to try and change what I could for the guy as much as it relied on me, by working with him towards a trio of big personal goals.

As we stood near the staircase, K shuffled over to me, as if it was a great effort to keep upright. I was to learn that indeed it was, as he was prone to losing his balance, mainly because of the toll a daily diet of alcohol had done to him over the years. K's paranoia was clear as he looked around him while we spoke, quietening if neighbours walked past. He told me how he regularly had dealers and other unwanted visitors knocking at his door most evenings, and he would only answer through the letterbox, *"Who is it?!"*, usually to no reply and the sound of shuffling away. He was in terrible fear of being broken into. The block where he lived was a known drugs haunt and quite an undesirable location to live. Whenever I saw the address come up on the system, it dawned on me that flats became vacant for one of two reasons: tenants were desperate to move out, or they had died in the meantime. I had learnt very quickly not to enter his flat for one very simple reason; K was an exceptionally heavy smoker and the air was so thick with it that my clothes would reek of stale tobacco, and passive smoking was not a pleasure. Not pleasant for me nor any of my other clients. K also disclosed to me a secret yearning; he had ditched his studies at university a couple of decades previously and dropped out because of falling into bad company and becoming addicted to alcohol. He wanted to resume studying if at all possible, because he had an aching to be a doctor. I was both fascinated and impressed.

However, K was hooked on alcohol. He would start his day by vomiting at around 11 a.m. with a 3 litre bottle of cider and would get through a further two such bottles during the rest of the day. There was no way he could simply reduce or stop when I asked him: "It would kill me if I went cold turkey." His diet was specially GP-prescribed milkshakes which would ensure he had a modicum of sustenance, albeit in liquid form. Here was a man who was literally holding on. He would often stumble in front of me, and had multiple medical issues including breathlessness/ COPD and blood complications. At such a comparatively young age this showed me the importance of looking after your body. There was one major thing that K needed to happen. He needed a 'detox'. A medical detox, a bit like a Keith Richards blood-change, but the proper one where you are interviewed, kept tabs on, reviewed and eventually admitted to a series of residential stays at a specialist alcohol unit, before the final operation. I joined the party about six months into the process and stayed in regular contact with the case workers. In order to ensure that the detox would work, K needed one extra thing which was my forte: a flat-move, anywhere quiet, away from temptations and free from interference. His reasoning was that the whole process would be undone if he was to return to his old flat with its memories and old haunts nearby. This was to take about two and a half years. In that time I would call him a couple of times per week, speak to his GP or his alcohol caseworkers on the odd occasion to check how things were progressing, have personal visits to check in with him, but mainly I would bid for new homes for him, and collect supporting evidence with which to make applications to the local authority, so as to get him up the ladder and into a higher priority housing banding based upon his medical needs. He was to be his own worst enemy. Even his first year of university was to amount to nothing, as sadly there were no official records of his study, after weeks of my investigation. As we finally secured him a flat subject to various lettings conditions and pleading with the housing association on his behalf, he became unnerved and was in two minds as to proceeding or not. I could not and would not allow this to completely lose all my hard work right at the last second. Rightly or wrongly, I was to speak frankly and brutally to him to make him realise the enormity of his decision: "*As you know, I'm leaving in two weeks' time. All my work with you has centred on getting you moved out of here so that your detox might work. If you don't go ahead with this flat now, you will lose it, you will have to stay put as you have changed your mind on other properties too, and this will almost certainly be the last chance you have to move. They will look at it as though you don't really need to be on this banding and you're not so serious a medical condition after all. My advice is to say 'yes' to me now, and I'll organize the last bits and pieces. Do not blow it all now!*"

He understood the reality and quietly gave me the OK. Right at the last available second with a caller awaiting the decision on the other phone line, we got him moved. I was not to see him achieve his detox. If truth be told, I have no idea whether K is still with us or not. So much in the balance.

How could a man my age, take such a different pathway that would lead him to throw his life away for a cheap dose of escapism that now held him hostage?

Truth and honesty

Now I'm no expert on addiction, although I have had a few training courses on the subject. What I have come across is a willful need to not only consume, but to self-destruct, as deep-down one of the root causes is often self-loathing.

It is an escape. It anaesthetises. It's also a trap. Once on that wheel you have to keep running. Running until your heart stops, unless you find a way out in time.

I don't think I ever came across much honesty with these gentlemen. It's as if the truth was not a good mixer with the spirit. Whatever good I might have achieved by furthering a financial claim, helping with a medical problem or organising specialist intervention, as soon as I closed the front door, departing into the winter air, I knew that they would be back to it and there was nothing I could do about it. I felt like a sticky plaster, a temporary solution to a long-term state of affairs, where time was relentlessly ticking one way....

Chapter Four

Captives of the past

It's one thing to look back and nod to what's been before as a reference point, but quite another to set up camp there. Some men are prisoners of the past as if an unseen mysterious hand is holding them back, a ghostly chain that only lets them go so far, before pulling them back to the bleak cell wall behind. After a while, that cell wall can start to feel comfortable...

Railway Man

Once upon a time, in a beautiful semi-rural setting, overlooking trees, a village and meadows, there lived by himself a man who enjoyed his garden and was content with life and at peace with the world.

This however was no fairy tale. He was once a retail professional, entrusted with store management and staff development, but he had since lost his way. As an only child, he had enjoyed a secure traditional upbringing, and was respectful of others. His father had been a proud man who gave little away emotionally, and he had been devoted to his mother. He loved the railways and as a boy would sometimes ride on the board with the steam loco drivers, as his uncle worked on the lines. *L's* life had fallen apart a couple of years prior to me meeting him. His mother with whom he lived in his childhood village had died of cancer, and he had no one to turn to while the bank took what little he had away. He told me he at that time he had nothing to his name, no job, no income, no house, no furniture and no hope. He had tried twice to end his life and was referred to the service to help him rebuild some normality, some structure and some semblance of a life worth living. He would speak fondly of a doctor who had championed his cause vigorously and somewhat exclusively, which made present GPs look uncaring and insensitive in comparison. You would never have known that my client was deeply depressed.

I remember that his home was immaculate, filled with ornaments, furniture and pristine décor. You couldn't move for furniture, but however tasteful, his home felt flooded with it, as if his furniture reflected what was going on inside him. In his kitchen was a glass dining table set for six in an elaborate hotel fashion, but not once would it ever see people gathered around it for celebration. There were pictures and frames proclaiming 'Love' and other sentiments which belied the anxious feelings he would hold under the surface. This was a home of tensions, held in a fine balance. He was enslaved to the system of benefits for those with mental health disabilities, relying on the income that was assessed on his mental and physical capabilities. On the other side, structured routines gave him comfort. His health was unpredictable, and he would suffer from mini strokes (TIAs), blackouts and very high blood pressure. We would go to the supermarket weekly, and if I was feeling productive, I might be able to sort out any of the latest pressing problems by phone, enroute. Much of the fresh food would be thrown out as his depression meant he couldn't face eating, often for several days at a time. Most often I felt like a counsellor, as I absorbed more and more-involved stories of the week's events and was asked about how I would deal with them if it were *me*.

In my time supporting him, I would see another dimension to his life; L had lost contact with his daughter for the majority of her life, having felt he had to walk away from his marriage. His daughter had been denied bedtime stories, tickling and the love of a father. He told me he had been more or less forced to leave, and over the years she had been force fed a false narrative about the type of man he was. He was happy to be in contact with her again and she seemed to be stable, married and well-adjusted. However, L spoke of agreeing to give her gifts of money in quite sizeable sums and he wondered if her husband knew of this as he would often be away. He would also show me texts and letters asking what I thought, as she would berate him for living the life he had, with no material assets such as a house for inheritance purposes. I could see both sides; his anguish and hers, competing for the best argument. In many ways they were both right. Each of them had missed out on each other. In the meantime, *L* just lived the best he could daily, and I felt that he was always so close to achieving various breakthroughs, yet so far too, as if it might be more comfortable to live with what you know, however painful, than to take a risk to find the possibilities of a brighter unknown. He's still on the rails, still sticking to his schedule and not yet run out of steam.

Could it be that we never really escape our pasts, or is it how we view the present and the future that really shapes our outlook on life?

Greek gangster

D was perhaps the most complicated of all of the men I used to support and represent. His sadness had followed him like a tracking hound all the way through his life, and he couldn't escape the pangs of feeling like an orphan even in his late sixties. He had been abandoned at the age of four, given away by his own mother to his grandparents who abused him, so that he ran away as a young man aged fourteen and became a stowaway on a ship, ending up in Canada and eventually, England. He never knew him properly, but his father was a British soldier, and although we tried, we never found him.

When I called *D* for the first time, he told me he was happy enough not to be visited as he was going to see a friend in London. After a couple more successive wellbeing check phone calls, he admitted to me that he didn't know anyone in London, and he was just embarrassed to disclose anything about his life. He let me visit him and it was then that I started to get a proper understanding of his circumstances. He was clinically obese and lived his life in semi-squallor, sleeping on a sofa that had a permanent slump in the middle. The sofa was where he sat, ate and slept, and this is key. Because he refused to recline, he would sleep every single day in a sitting position which inflamed his legs and excessive fluid in the tissues massively engorged them. He took tablets for this infirmity, but those legs were the most grotesquely swollen I had seen: the medical term is *'peripheral edema'*. He once fell and I nearly broke my back trying to lift him up to his feet.

His front room was his bedroom, living room and dining room all rolled into one. Old dinner plates, bottles of *Coca Cola*, *Bells* and *Famous Grouse* littered the room, which had debris strewn across it. In front of his sofa was placed a coffee table which housed all the necessaries like roll-ups, tobacco, lighters and paperwork. This was an organized set-up in the middle of a complete mess, which he explained to me. He had everything important arranged close to the sofa, almost like it had been in his prison cell. Prison had given him order. He had been sent down for thirteen years for being a part of a Heathrow Airport armed robbery. (The mention of an airport I had worked at got me interested.) Prison had not left his psyche however, and he lived each day as though he was in a cell of his own making. His whiskey intake was up to six litre-bottles per week. He was a chronic hoarder, collecting high value goods and trinkets which he didn't have a use for, but there was his compulsive habit, accumulation. He used to be a street artist, once having had a beautiful girlfriend whom he mistreated by driving away as he hated himself deep inside. He used to tell me what he thought I wanted to hear; like his whiskey intake had gone down. Of course, it never truly did.

D had also been the victim of a medical operation that had gone wrong, and as a result, he received compensation to the tune of several hundred thousand pounds. He admitted to me that he had spent all of it on items he would never use, like prestige *Nikon* cameras, first generation *Apple* computers and *Samsung* tablets, all of which remained in packaging, covered in a sheen of dust. He would beg me to be careful around his flat for the sake of knocking things over like ornate glass sculptures, yet the carpet was mainly obscured with dirty plates, discarded letters, batteries, and anything he had thrown away from the sofa in temper. On many occasions he would ask me to throw away the rubbish from the kitchen and the living room, as well as the recycling. His bin bags would be heavy from glass whiskey bottles. Sometimes, flies would hover above the bin in his living room. I was to understand that the polyethene supermarket bags he would ask me to remove would contain his excrement, and the flies gave the game away. I would remove them without fuss.

D could be a Jekyll and Hyde character, one moment courteous and even buoyant, the next, fed up with life and angry at the world. An office colleague joining me for a day was astounded at the vitriolic way *D* spoke to me. I understood that his prison experience had coloured his worldview. He had somehow felt safer behind bars but now no longer felt that same protection in his own flat and every noise or knock at his front door would remind him of his own vulnerability. He couldn't protect himself. He told me that he would never move from his flat, and that the only way he would leave was if he was carried out. He would sometimes weep, his head resting on his chest, sobbing heavily, feeling shameful at what he had become, and what had happened to him. He would sometimes refer to his mother: *"My own mother gave me away as a child... she did this to me...how could she?!"* That pain had followed him everywhere.

It took longer than I thought it would for *D*'s body to finally give out, but two and a half years later, I would drive past to see his ground floor flat windows open, the net curtains removed. As promised, he would only leave that flat one way. I knew in that instant that he had been carried out. And all his precious possessions? I heard they had all been chucked onto a flatbed truck and dumped.

What exactly had broken inside this gentleman to make him so thwarted and self-destructive? Had he carried that childhood abandonment all through his life? Was finding his father the key to it all?

Confined to the tracks...

V was one of those likeable men who happened to suffer from anxiety and an obsession with the past. He lived his life in the same house he had lived in with his parents before they passed on, but still the décor was stuck in the seventies. He craved a partner to share life with, but never found one willing to accept him, or more certainly that he dared risk asking. Just like the locomotives of yesteryear, his pathway was confined to the tracks he knew and nothing more.

V had been through a succession of support workers and told a story so compelling of hard honest manual toil, that you felt here was a polite and honest man who was somewhat lost and often ridiculed. His front room and his kitchen looked like they had hardly changed in decades, as though interfering with, or updating the décor would interfere with the past too much. He collected biscuit tins, gravy tins and chocolate tins on a shelf in the kitchen where they were rusting happily. His pay as you go mobile would usually have no credit on it, but he would cautiously let you know the impressive amount of savings he had, and how maybe others would be jealous. He would ride a mountain bike everywhere, as long as 'everywhere' was within no more than a two- mile radius of his house. The only out-of-town experiences he would have, would be with his sister and brother-in-law every Friday, usually at a café near one of two railway museums. I even tried to put him in touch with 'Railway Man' on account of their shared love of steam trains gone by, but their exchanges were polite and short-lived. He would regularly recite the names of all the support workers he had been given who had kept him stable through his years of anxiety disorder. This 'mantra' would be his prop to show how many had invested in him. He was a man it was impossible to dislike.

Things started to get interesting when he was targeted by local drug dealers and 'friends' seeing him as a soft touch. Just like vampires begging to be let in through the door, they would wait until dark before preying on their victim, using a female purr through the letterbox to let them in. While she distracted him, they managed to go through his upstairs rooms and steal coins from his kitchen table that he had piled up to pay his weekly bedroom-tax. As I uncovered more information back at base, I understood the names of certain local villains would be repeated almost as if they were celebrities, well-known to the housing provider's ASB team as well as by the police. No sooner than I had found out, I started to organise the security measures we would need to ensure his safety. I worked hard to empower him.

V could sometimes be his own worst enemy, and in an unfortunate twist, fell victim to a neighbour who had been taunting him and goading him for several years. Unable to restrain himself following an episode of anatagonising, he loudly mouthed off in the garden about what he'd like to do to said-neighbour, only to find himself with an official police-visit and warning. The neighbour had slyly been recording him and it was committed to phone memory and used as evidence against the man with less ability to cope with these things... *V* was mortified and deeply embarrassed. He was now on a warning-list.

Life would coast along, until one day when I received an-out-of-the blue phone call from a nurse at the city's hospital. *V* had been cycling down his familiar streets when one of his pedals had come off, causing him to topple into the road in front of a bus. He wasn't run over but suffered a complex head injury and was taken to hospital. They thought to call me to ask if he was usually this way, as they were putting him through tests and were a little concerned over his responsiveness. I chuckled as I replied he was mostly like this. I would receive a call within three days to tell me that he had passed away, aged 64. His body was riddled with uncurable cancer and the compression ultimately took his life. As his sister and brother-in-law went from room to room at his now unoccupied childhood home, they shook their heads in disbelief. What saddened me, was that here was a man who had never truly *lived* but was always in the shadows of what might happen, even down to finding love. Whenever I pass by that railway museum and see all those vintage carriages on the sidings, I think of him.

What joy might he have found if he had been more willing to take risks in finding love and life beyond his childhood boundaries?

Cabaret to care home

It started off easily enough with absolutely nothing to suggest the despair that it would end up being. On the same street as Greek Gangster, there lived a slender elderly man whose high theatrical kicks impressed me as much as his artistic abilities. B was 92 and you would absolutely never have believed it. (72 would have fooled you.) Living on his own in a Georgian flat, but with a zest for life and a faithful group of friends, B was always dressed immaculately and always treated me to the luxury branded chocolate biscuits whenever I visited. He needed simple check-up visits, some small talk and my help with getting to the bottom of extremely high bills from a gas provider. Yes, *that* gas provider. It took me a few weeks of visits, calls, emails, photos of the meter, arranging appointments to change it and finally to get his refund in place of nearly £700, and thereon accurate bills. B didn't know what to say, which was fine. It was all part of the service.

He took great pleasure in showing me his old photo albums and a 'book' he had put together of his life containing memoirs, theatre shows (plenty of make-up) and love and losses. He told me that when he married in the seventies, he couldn't consummate the relationship. I got thinking; *'How could his wife not tell he was gay?'* They had obviously not slept together until the night of their wedding day. (Nowadays the norm is to do that on the first or second date. Shows you how times have changed. Just a social comment.) He told me of a Russian boy he had fallen in love with, but they couldn't be together. He stroked the photos longingly. It was obviously painful for him to talk about, but there were others he alluded to. They were all mentioned in his memoirs.

Out of the blue, I received a near emotional phone call from one of his worried friends who seemed to think that I as *'B's social worker* and *representative of the local authority'* (neither of which was strictly true) had a responsibility to come immediately to deal with B. I managed to get into his flat, meeting the friend there. B was in bed. He was dehydrated, pale, skeletal and paralysed by mental anguish. I had not seen this before, as I had only been supporting *B* for a few months, and he was an expert at putting on a wonderful *'life is a cabaret'* mask, but he was nothing like Liza Minelli or Michael York. I found a list of friends beside his phone and gaining consent I phoned the lady who knew him best. She explained it with two words: Winter depression. It turned out it was seasonal and as regular as clockwork. He was lamenting his life, his lost loves and his loneliness. The ambulance was called, and they attended. While they were dealing with him, I looked about the flat for clues. His fridge was nearly empty, he was malnourished by his own will and I was informed that he rarely washed. You would never have known this as he always presented himself well. (Masks. I'll talk about these later on.) This depression carried on for many weeks and suffice to say there was much professional intervention. I got a jovial specialist social worker and her team on board. It gave a welcome comedic balance to the sobriety whenever I spoke with her. It was arguable that he had capacity and now he needed others to safeguard him. It was during this time that I realised he knew one of my family members, so to maintain client confidentiality I had to keep anything I knew strictly to myself. Difficult but not impossible.

I managed to contact his niece who lived 100 miles away and she came to visit to keep an eye on him. He gave the impression he was eating properly but was a theatrical master of disguise. Just as *B* seemed to be getting better, I went to visit him one late morning and he toppled over in weak confusion, grabbing my arm as he fell flat. I called the ambulance immediately, he ended up in hospital and that was the beginning of the end of his tenancy there. He never returned. We found a funding stream for short-term extra care which saw him moved out of his impressive urban grandeur and into a self-contained room with countryside views. It was to see him through to the end of life. His niece had packed his essentials which included his memoirs of course. He never did manage a high kick for me again, but it's still making me smile as I look out of my kitchen window. What a gas....

Maisonette mistrust

I rang the doorbell to the flat having walked just off the main street and into a foyer where it split into two sides: turn left for a business and to the right, a main door for several flats. It was one of several joint visits with repairs men and local authority building-control managers. Our elderly man (my new client) lived on the top floor and greeted us at the door cautiously and suspiciously through his glasses. My job was to ensure his interests and his mental health were being looked after. In his twilight years, my client was as prickly as a pufferfish, moaning loudly at the slightest move we made to check the state of the roof, kitchen, bathroom, living room and bedroom. It was all an extremely sorry sight. I had not come across such décor since my formative years. It was just as if someone had pressed 'pause' in 1973, and then 'play' four decades later, but with all the associated decay. It was a flat that was owned by the council but managed by the housing provider.

It didn't take me longer than a couple of minutes to work out why it was in such a bad brown way with rot, dry rot, damp and antiquated systems. My client would not allow anyone in, fearing that he would be robbed again of his possessions as he claimed he had been on other occasions. Anyone entering the flat would have been aware of the smoke engrained on the threadbare carpets, the dark rooms where curtains had been drawn through the summer and piles of uncertain belongings resting on top of ancient gas heaters and old bed frames. There was only one thing stopping us from giving my client a virtually brand new, fixed, redecorated, clean and homely fit for purpose flat: himself. What I didn't reckon on was how much of a battle this would be. His fixation was the ruined TV signal and aerial interfered with by seagulls, which he went to great technical lengths to describe. (I realised once again how important a friend the TV is for lonely and vulnerable persons.)

I also discovered something else about my client which if true, tells you that everyone has a story, a background and a reason as to why they are like they are, for better or for worse. He had worked hard all his life for the council, as the public convenience cleaner (WC) for the entire blocks in the city. That was his main job for decades. I had to stop and give him credit for that alone. He was full of mistrust for anyone save my colleague who had passed him onto me. I sensed his anxiety. There was something else though. He had told something to a former colleague who gave me this information a couple of weeks after hand-over to me, and it had all been verified by dates, research and letters of confirmation. He was the son of a very famous and debonair forties and fifties Hollywood actor. However this was not public knowledge in any way and was kept secret entirely. He was what tabloid papers refer to as 'a lovechild'. As I write this, I am open-mouthed. I thought I would look up images for myself and found an old stock one on the internet of the actor's father. There stood a hard-working man in a garden, resplendent in black waistcoat with pocket watch, trousers, white shirt and fag in mouth, the *identical match* with my client. That man in the photo would have been my client's grandfather. No-one would ever know as this secret would go to the grave. (You're probably trying to think who that actor was. It would be Indiscreet of me to say.)

The saddest bit for me was that I would not see this case to fruition. My client and I had strong words over the phone, as it was my belief that he didn't need appeasing, he needed to play ball with us. The flat was beyond urgent need of repair for his own safety, and the only way it could be done was to move him out into another flat temporarily. He would not have it at all, and I was to become the enemy because I was giving him the truth, for time was running out and I wanted a result for him and with him. He put his foot down and maintained the only reason people wanted him out of his flat was to rob him blind. I had to bail out and pass him onto another colleague as he wouldn't work with me at all. He was to end up in hospital I discovered a couple of months later. Somehow I got the message that he wanted me to look after his budgie while he was away. I felt a little heartless by declining, but to be put under the spotlight if he claimed anything went missing...? Me under Suspicion: some things just ain't worth it.

It struck me with all these gentlemen that it's a reminder to all of us of how quickly life can change, but to make the most of each day, as *'carpe diem'* rings in my ears. As I write, only one of these men remains with us.

A cemetery for a home

This is a tag-on story that I only just remembered but it made sense to put it here. I was called one day as one of our customers had been overlooked for months by changes in workers and had not even had a wellbeing check phone call. I was asked by my manager to urgently call him ASAP to restore his confidence in the service. I was bracing myself for a severe backlash, but what I actually got was a really amiable gentleman with a sense of humour you only get from age and a lifetime's service to the council, who just needed some help. I asked him how I could intervene. He had lived with his wife in a cemetery lodge, a gothic looking building at the gates of one of the local churches, which I had only ever given the odd glance at whenever driving past. They had enjoyed about 30 years there, but his wife had passed away a few years back and he was now on his own, with thoughts tormenting him, unable to make it up and down the stairs to have a bath in months. (Don't worry, he managed to wash himself daily in other ways.) He needed to move but wasn't holding out much hope, as the other workers hadn't managed anything in the last year. I told him to watch this space and to start packing, as I would get things rolling that day. He was now in my care, and I sensed he was tentatively hopeful. He swore casually and for this I liked him.

Pulling as many strings as my paygrade would allow, I got him registered onto the system as a priority case through a useful contact, asked where he would consider moving to and lined up several sheltered property options within a mile or two of his current home. Liaising with his daughter who worked for a law firm, I was able to iron out any hiccups and expedite the solution. The usual time frame for a move like this would be three to six months. Within just eight short weeks, he was out of that dark three-bedroom lodge with its tomb of memories. When I asked him how he was getting on in his new home, he replied: *"I'm as happy as a pig in shit! I can't believe it; I've waited years for this and in you come and you get me sorted almost immediately!"*

I met him for the first and only time in his new one bed bungalow. He could now shower happily, was self-contained with his broadband set up, and had sufficient garden space around to keep him occupied. He plied me with enough cake and coffee to keep a broken man happy. He was no longer a prisoner of the past with a view of the tombstones. His story had a happy ending in a mini-paradise. I loved results like this, and it still makes me smile just thinking about it. You might even say I was dead proud of myself.

Chapter Five

Dependencies

When one thing is dependent upon another... When you build a working relationship with vulnerable people and they open up their lives for you to come in and experience what they are going through, then you create a rapport, an empathy and a desire to do the best by them. They don't become your friends, but they do become your lookout. There can often be a dependency upon you to make anything happen.

A father's blueprint for his son

H was an outwardly likeable young man in his early thirties, who was referred to me to help support with basic financial issues mainly and a big problem which wouldn't go away. He couldn't hold down his tenancy mainly because he had a personality disorder, medically diagnosed by the Mental Health Team. He would over-react when goaded by neighbours upstairs who well-knew the thin ice he was already skating on. I would have to work harder still to keep his tenancy secure even though it was heading for the courts and stood little chance of appeal. He had a voracious sexual appetite and it was uncomfortable to listen to him as he would relay what he would like to do to said lady upstairs who was apparently giving him the come-on at every opportunity. He lived in a world of his own.

It was his mother I felt for. She was not only working full time and running her own household, but also doing everything she could to keep him away from trouble and fall into traps he couldn't see coming. These traps ranged from entering mobile phone contracts he couldn't afford and being tied into excessive penalties, to breaching the tenancy agreement of his nearby flat on several key clauses. It wasn't that he was physically incapable of working, for he was a strong physical specimen. It was his mental outlook and his psychosis which would prove his downfall. He simply didn't have the capacity to fully understand the implications of anything he did. His mother would handle his benefits money and give him a daily allowance; this was the only sure way things might work.

On one of my visits, he showed me a picture of his little girl and his ex-girlfriend who was now happily married and living far away. He had stayed there once on a weekend visit, but realised he was not cut out to be a dad, so left another man to bring up his daughter in a secure family. He told me about his own father and how difficult it had been to get to know him because he was an alcoholic, abusive and not present when they needed him. He had walked out on his family and died when *H* was young, leaving his mother to raise him.

Meanwhile, I was busy liaising with a specialist criminal solicitor to try to assist in his defence in the case brought against him by the housing provider, which also happened to be my employer. Just as we were starting to address some issues and possibly hold onto his flat through medical professionals' intervention and dialogue with the tenancy team, he shot himself in the foot badly. Having gone out for some beers one afternoon, he followed an elderly lady and approaching her from behind, loudly told her what he would like to do to her. Apparently, she called the police as well as the housing provider and eventually me. Of *all* the ladies he could have chosen, she was also one of my clients. She was shaken so badly by this incident that she could now no longer trust a male and was passed over understandably to one of my female colleagues. Two years of my work with this lady, battling her corner and issues, were now down the drain.

It soon came to the point where I was in an obvious conflict of interests. It seemed like I was the only person who might stand in the way of the inevitable. As much as the Mental Health Team manager wanted me to better-advocate our mutual client, such was the level of evidence against *H*, that I could not stand against the court process of eviction, which is where this was heading. Internal advice was given to me to stand down. I had to relay this to his mother. Understandably she was angry and questioned whether or not I had actually done anything whilst I had been in their 'employment'. I went through a short list of successes, but we had to draw a line underneath this, and I bowed out reluctantly. One thing we had talked about in-depth was his father, how he had been denied a good strong role-model and sadly had been given the opposite. No-one to show him the right way. A blueprint for how not to be.

How many fathers are so broken themselves, that they can't see the negative blueprints they set will outlive them and cause hurts for the next generations?

Food and mental health: an unhealthy relationship

This doesn't follow for everyone but it's pretty much a given that when you're 'off your food', it's always for a reason. You're usually either sick or worried. For men who live alone, to eat by yourself is normal. I always found it quite mechanical. Meals tend to make more sense when you're eating with someone, as they're an act of togetherness, fellowship and even celebration. If you over-eat, that's usually for a reason too, mainly to satisfy something that you can't satisfy any other way. I have seen it too as an act of self-loathing. (Four doughnuts in a row is my limit.)

It astounded me that when my client regularly discarded perfectly good food into the bin, he had abandoned sense and followed a reasoning all of his own. The sell-by dates had passed, but there was something final about the act of throwing away, as though it was a ritual which had to be obeyed. He would not eat for several days as though he was teaching his body a lesson, that he could subdue it and that he could willfully destroy it if he had to. I genuinely worried for him but there was little I could do.

There is so much written about eating disorders that I won't add anything scientific to this part. On a practical level, you might know of someone who is going through this self-denial. All I can say, is that eating with others helps your mental health immeasurably. We weren't designed to eat alone.

Cut down

It was thought that I would be a good match to G - being a musician- and could best serve this gentleman, who was a shameless name-dropper, having played with musicians with direct lines to rock royalty. His drumming was basic but with a tinge of colour, a little like his lifestyle. He would open up to me and say; *"Simon, I need a muse to come and look after me.....!"* He had previously enjoyed an aristocratic upbringing, mixed with transatlantic living which was sent down to earth with a solid bump in a suburban housing estate where fly-tipping, shouting and good humour mixed comfortably.

I started the ball rolling with addressing some pensions problems. He had spent many years in the USA previously, and was now estranged from his wife and children, and had not seen them in several years. A family court had ruled that he should pay maintenance to his wife for the upbringing of their children- a decree that he had no problem with. However, the unusual situation was that he was receiving a pension from the USA and was also eligible for a UK pension, but could not open a bank account in the USA so his funds would remain there, without travelling all the way over there. He could not afford the air-fare or the passport and had not the will to fly. He was also keeping something from me and everyone else, that he would not reveal until he absolutely had to.

The DWP (*Department of Work & Pensions*) had decided that he was now no longer entitled to *Pension Credit*- a state top-up to allow a liveable income- and this was impacting on his ability to wire money back to the States, which he did at his own cost, coming to approximately £20 a time, just for the privilege of doing so from his local Post Office. Honourably, he would still send across the full amount to his family and take the hit of the postage on himself. The DWP were also claiming a repayment from him, backdating it several months. I contacted the US pensions service in this country as well as in the USA and got nowhere. It left him in the position of being unable to afford normal life, and we had to look at the foodbank just to make it through. (Even his rusty cooker was on its last legs and I managed to secure a grant for a new model that made him beam with joy as the electrics were connected by a tradesman.) I contacted the DWP to start an appeal process and put my lawyer-head on, on his behalf explaining his MH issues, the whole scenario about the pensions complications and his estrangement from his family across the pond. He had not had any contact from his daughter in several years who was now an adult. I also took the Pension Credit issue to the local MPs office as a high priority, albeit a very unusual case. The MP escalated it for me to the House of Lords and within a couple of weeks, G excitedly called me. Despite having been turned down for an appeal, he was more impressed that the negative decision in an official letter had come from none other than the Minister for Pensions himself, *Lord Freud*. I told him, "G, we can go no higher!"

News broke one day when his 19-year old son in the sunshine state had been caught stealing a bicycle, and to avoid a custodial sentence based on other issues, intervention was urgently required by an attorney. He had no state legal aid, and the lawyer looking to act on his behalf was after $5,000. His son visited that summer, but apparently was arrested on return to the USA as he had broken bail conditions. We worked hard to get this overturned by calling and emailing the local law enforcement agencies and the efficient state-appointed attorney.

On top of this, G no longer slept in his own bedroom as a cross-dresser next door would wail, shout, bang and crash all night, forcing G to sleep on his sofa. I got the housing provider involved as well as the Mental health services, reporting the situation as best as I could. One day I received an urgent call that G had tripped on a pothole out in the street. The ambulance had tended to him and he was heavily bruised on his head and his leg. He beseeched me to contact a personal accident solicitor and I relayed the story. We took it so far, by looking at a negligence claim for damages against the Highways department before he asked me not to proceed anymore. The reason? My service was being funded by the same local authority whom he was considering suing. I could see the irony and his sense of justice, agreeing to metaphorically shake hands and write this one off to experience. There was however, one thing that *G* was keeping from us all: he was dying of cancer. This was delicate. My job was never straightforward.

Reconciliation came relatively speedily with his family, including his wife. Within a few weeks, specialist intervention came from professionals within cancer charities, as well as the NHS, via his GP and the local hospital. I felt like an add-on. A vital link, but still an add-on. Cancer-specialist nurses and his GP were present as I visited on one Wednesday morning. "How long has he got?" I asked the nurse as we spoke discreetly in his kitchen. She gave him a few days at most. 48 hours later, I was at his bedside in the cancer ward, reading *Psalm 23* out loud to him whilst he slept, breathing through an oxygen mask. It was perhaps too obvious a Psalm, but lost sheep always need a shepherd, so it was just what he needed to hear. (A year or so earlier, he had become irate when he had espied my wife's Bible in the car as I gave him a lift into town, ranting about God not caring, before calming down and admitting he had given his life to JC back in the States as a younger man.) Second time I had been in that hospital ward giving someone I knew well the message of hope. He startled me when he suddenly came around, removed his oxygen mask and blurted out, "What's happening to all my stuff?!" (His expensive guitars, smart TV and various iproducts must have been greatly on his mind, even at his journey's end...) I told him to rest and forget about his stuff. When I checked in with his family by phone on the Monday morning, his long-suffering sister-in-law broke the expected news that he had passed away on the Saturday night with his family at his bedside. It was still a sad moment.

Cue the funeral a week or so later, and the crematorium was packed. I sat quietly near the back. As the throng left, I made a beeline for the vicar who shook my hand vigorously as apparently she had heard a lot about me. She looked sadly at me, telling me how hard humanist funerals were like this, so final and with no hope of redemption beyond. I gave her the better news that the deceased actually did have a hope, and she practically jumped for joy. If just for that moment of surrender all those years earlier to a Saviour he had not seen, yet believed in, then ironically, it looked like G had more hope than most of those at the funeral.

Left to his own devices

With his beloved dog at his side, A had ended up in a wheelchair as a result of a larger man sitting on him and breaking his back. He had- in a short space of time- lost all his belongings, his old home and especially any hope of a decent future.

As I helped him navigate his life, it was obvious that however much he protested, he could not organise his home nor his finances properly, and my intervention was often needed as electricity was cut off, benefits payments stopped, letters of authority demanded, and GP intervention called for. Left to his own devices and his own will, sadly A could not cope. Like an ostrich that buries its head in the sand, so was my client with his basic outgoings and budgeting. His way of dealing with it was to shout above the sounds of arguing on *The Jeremy Kyle Show,* exclaiming how he was an intelligent man and why everyone else was on his back was a mystery. We waited in a virtual queue for about 18 months, before his *Disabled Facilities Grant* (DFG) materialised, which enabled his specially adapted kitchen and shower room to be fitted. His childlike happiness was never far away. The shine on his face from something so simple as an egg and bacon sandwich was a joy. Here was a simple man with simple needs. (If you think I'm being patronising, I'm not; it's only because I recognise this similarity in myself.)

I could often leave him week to week with just a check-up call which sometimes he would answer, and sometimes not. I was sure he thought I didn't understand any of what he was going through, but the truth was I knew more than I gave away. My hands were tied until I got a green light to act.

It was going to be a couple of years before the real work reared its head. Two strands of problems had emerged to the point that they needed immediate intervention to stop harm. The first was that he claimed a close family member was stealing cash from him, and this was corroborated by a lady-friend he knew in a neighbouring block of flats. The family member was a known offender who could not handle their own life properly, and probably saw anyone else as rich pickings, even a vulnerable relative. The second issue was at least equal in magnitude; somehow, he had accumulated a backlog of several thousand pounds of unpaid council tax, which was not only enough to put his tenancy in jeopardy, but also to send him straight to court and possibly jail. I was only alerted to the latter by a department-head colleague in Rents who asked me if I still supported him, and then she explained the severe financial state of affairs. These problems were to occur in my last few months as his advocate, and involved the police, safeguarding professionals and myself primarily, to stabilize and agree with A some way of protecting him and moving forward. However, he decided that even though he needed protection, he would not be pressing any charges, as the relative was 'too close to home'.

I cannot say that his life will now be stable or these issues now over. All I know, is that like any of us, these things can come and go periodically, and resurface like a shark's tail suddenly becoming visible on the surface waters.

Slipped through the net

Guy gave me a lift up the hill out of the city and we sat outside a block of flats which was a scheme belonging to another housing provider. As usual, he quickly briefed me on the background and current needs of this client, before we left the car and rang the doorbell. With tattoos and piercings, this gentleman could seem intimidating, but was younger than most of the others. He was one of those who was most in need and would have slipped though the net for the adult social care funding-criteria, had it not been for petitioning.

His speech was slurred but it was not from alcohol but appeared to be the after-effects of years of self-abuse. He needed some adaptations to his bathroom to make bathing easier, and this element alone took about two years to organise with me putting his argument forward with OTs and Adult Social Care.

B had lost his once-comfortable life through succumbing to hard drugs and although he poured out his heart, I was never quite sure about what was *really* going on. He always sounded stoned but probably wasn't, as there was never any evidence around. His ex-partner had left him destitute, with four-figure water bills alone as well as other priority debts, and the heart-aching feeling that he would never see his growing boys again. He would sit on his sofa and I could almost see the pain exuding from him, as he told me he would sometimes watch them from the school fence with other parents, just to glimpse them from afar as they finished their school day. He claimed to see disturbing visions in the middle of the night, which made me look at the flat in a different way. The debts such as council tax, water and TV licence prompted me to immediately get CAB involved. As usual in flats, there was always a form of antagonism and borderline ASB going on as he told me about the odd argument with neighbours. B let it slip one day that he had been sitting down one day fiddling about with a piece of rope while he watched TV. Subconsciously he had fashioned a noose. It shocked him when he looked down at it, but he told me he had a suicide plan; it was *where* and *how*, but he just needed the *when*. That never came on my watch.

I became lightly involved with the legal side by liaising with a family law firm just to chase up matters on his behalf, but it appeared the solicitor and barrister were doing an exemplary job of fighting his side. No need for me to muscle in at all. Beyond this, it emerged that he had a difficult relationship with his father. All the while that B was battling the legal system to see his sons, he eventually discovered his father had access to them ahead of him. He was understandably furious. I was to leave before I ever saw fruition to this situation, but he seemed to live his life upkeeping his flat as a distraction to the obvious heart-wrenching going on inside.

How many men slip through the net like this? How many more have difficult relationships with their fathers?

Half the story

Although my visits to this retired gentleman were fairly straightforward on the surface, I believed not all was as it seemed. L couldn't read or write and relied on a very basic understanding of recognizing letters and familiar-looking words. Living with his elderly mother, and struggling with his physical health, he spent all his days inside watching old re-runs on satellite TV, as he couldn't face the sun, was very overweight and his favourite phrase was 'My doctor's not too happy with me...' Slurred speech in the afternoons suggested to me that he was not telling me the whole story.

My main job on visits was to go through the mail, paying special attention to the brown envelopes, containing pensions and benefits letters and re-applications. Sometimes he would give the appearance that he could manage finances well, while on other visits, he would seem to come apart at the seams. He would regularly enroll himself into those sales of mass-produced souvenirs like old vehicle models or commemorative stamps from magazine adverts and then not keep up with the payments. He was regularly scammed, and I could see the foundation to this was a combination of loneliness, missed opportunities, ill-health and a bondage to the past.

Although he was his mother's primary carer, he had input from local agencies, help with household chores and was attending the local college for reading and writing lessons. However, he could not manage a simple 200 metre walk to the newsagents up the road to get his morning paper, without breathing complications and many stops. He would often use the car instead.

I felt that inside him was probably a resignation to an untold sadness. Every day was the same, broken up by just a single change to the routine, like the bank, an outing, shopping or classes. He had rarely been out of the county, let alone the country. He seemed content to be absorbed into those old comedy programmes of his childhood, 80s and 90s films and dramas of yesteryear. He had never really broken free of his mother, nor found his own love and although he seemed content to press 'repeat' every day, I sensed he was barely living life at all. There was definitely something he wasn't telling me either. I suspected it might be some dark secret or craving. I would leave him to others to take over.

Play; Rewind; Repeat. Every day. Every month. Every decade.

Needle-park finger-pointer

For a few months, I supported a gentleman who seemed to have everything under control himself and was adept at pointing out the faults of others and the poor state of the immediate areas around his locality. *K* majored on showing me the overgrown boundary hedges on pathways, the fly-tipping behind the neighbouring blocks of flats and most notably drug-dealing. He told me the times and the days I should look out for. *K* had to be discreet himself for fear of reprisals, but he was right. Every Tuesday, Wednesday and Thursday like clockwork, morning until lunchtime, a succession of prestige cars would come and go, parking on pavements or blocking garages. He even saw a regular plastic bag drop from a third-floor balcony and the collection below. He also pointed out to me that if he wandered through the local playpark with his dog, he would often find junkies' needles there.

K was a prickly character as he was purely transactional. It was a case of '*What are you and your organisation going to do about it?*' When I went into his house, to complete some checks and fill in some paperwork with him, it was so thick with smoke, that I requested to stay near an open door to preserve my own lungs a little longer. The décor was dated, and he lived alone. Unsurprisingly, he had breathing difficulties. I figured that below the surface and beyond his professional abilities as a telecoms engineer, *K* was an unhappy soul. He preferred to keep it that way. A fixation with a needle-park and the state of the community areas would mean no-one need ever get close to the broken man inside, least himself.

If it's always someone else's fault, then it often starts with deflecting unwanted spotlights away from your own hidden areas...

Bullied into submission

Some people you meet in life are outwardly measured and well-ordered, whose lives are simple because they *have* to be. Here was a man who lived alone with his small dog in a quiet pristine ground floor flat which he had taken on as the result of a 'sensitive let' as known in housing circles: he was taken away from a threatening situation. *E* had been sufficiently bullied, belittled and beaten back into a corner. *E* was a pleasant man in his late forties who relied heavily on the routines of support from basic help with official phone calls where he would quickly unravel if left to his own devices, to sorting out his problems with yet more bullying, this time from some intimidating neighbours living in the flat upstairs. He had moved from his beautiful city-centre Georgian flat because he was in fear of a little man who used to indulge in domestic violence and intimidated the whole building. *E* also had one thing in common with so many men I supported: a difficult relationship with his dad, but a strong bond with his mother.

On a trio of occasions in the three and a half years of support, he had cried out for help as the inability to manage had become too much, and the overwhelming urge to end his life saw him scream at me one day that he was going to throw himself out of the window.... in front of me. Panic attack symptoms include rapid and shallow breathing (hyperventilation). It was real and could have been disturbing, had I not seen panic attacks before and the devastation they cause, for myself. We had to move him out of urgency. The new property was not to be so wonderful, despite his successful work on transforming it into a comfortable flat.

Drug dealing was carrying on several doors down and bearing in mind that *E* had been moved here on a sensitive let on account of his own mental health, this was the last thing he needed. I heard reports of multiples of men and women wandering through in hoodies usually, day and night, with parties, fires, cars screeching away and a whole host of questionable activities, not in keeping with a one-bedroomed flat. *E* had received a couple of visits from the dealing-tenant and had made it clear that he wanted nothing more than to keep himself to himself. I had done my own research and found out that *the dealer* was under more surveillance than I had given the authorities credit for.

At one point, the funding stream for all clients was altered which meant that (just like the British generals dividing Cyprus into two sides with a marker pen,) anyone under the age of 50 would no longer be entitled to support unless they paid out of their own pockets. His GP and I would regularly check in with each other as she used to tell me that the number of visits he made to her surgery would increase in times of uncertainty, so funding was imperative. He deemed this regularity of visits and check-ins so vital that he managed for a few weeks to borrow some money to keep a reduced level of contact going, until the funding stream was reinstated. (NB. The money was not paid directly to me, but to my employer of course.) *E* stuck it out as long as he could. It transpired he was suffering bullying coming from upstairs, noise during the night and intimidation. This seemed to be a pattern in his life. It goes back to that 'dog eat dog' scenario or 'survival of the fittest'. People can sense when someone is playing the victim and play on that. When the victim remains in victim-mode the circle is complete, and it carries on. We got the noise-measuring equipment organised and the sound levels were monitored over two weeks, but upstairs got wise to it and behaved themselves temporarily. I was not to see him leave the area, as that was to be after my time there. He had had enough. He was to not only leave the flat, but the entire county, to return to his childhood home far away from threats, disorder and instability.

Closed curtains

The social worker met me around the corner of the building to brief me quickly on my next client and what his needs were. M had been a logistics employee whose life had taken a turn. He was full of deep mistrust on the first meeting, which within a week or so, turned into a willingness to use my help.

An HGV accident had left him with certainly some trauma, but also intense back pain and a reliance on lager and wine just to start his days. His curtains were always closed, his speech slurred and a general slowness; my overriding memory of my brief time there at his flat. I didn't always trust the quality of his visitors, but that was his lookout. When he allowed natural light into his flat, there were pictures of a happier life gone by, of his family, his old life, a wife and child....

Council Tax, housing management problems and debt payments that had not been kept track of meant that M should have been in a better position. I helped by trying to get on top of his admin which unattended to, would have impacted his benefits payments negatively. That old phrase, 'you can lead a horse to water...' would have surmised M's position just right. Although I bought him more time with creditors and was making promises on his behalf, he just couldn't quite see the last bit through, which was to part with some cash in installments which I had negotiated. (This was not uncommon with many of my clients.) Some, like M, would just bury their heads in the sand hoping the problem would go away, as another drink would blank everything out. Momentarily.

I found him kitchen crockery and utensils, as well as a grant for a used washing machine and tumble dryer in my last 10 days. He was over the moon. He used to call me 'cool dude', which of course I liked. Just as I was starting to get somewhere, I would leave. Sadly, I knew I had only just scratched the surface.

The loner milkman

Working on behalf of this isolated retired gentleman in his sixties and in poor health, was arguably the finest example of inter-agency working the whole group had ever been involved in. We worked hard to move him out of a dangerous house, keep him safe both financially and physically, and eventually secure his inheritance via lawyers acting for the estate. He is now comfortable, healthier and happy. Here is how it started...

Living alone in his childhood home a house troubled by rats since his mother had passed away to cancer, *T* had been an ex-milk board employee. His had been a life of simplicity. He paid his weekly wages to his mother and she would look after everything else, so he had no concept of bills, responsibilities or how to run a home in the traditional sense. He kept himself to his slender self and walked the streets somewhat anonymously, blending in with others on life's daily bus trips and visits to the bank. He had intensive breathing problems and didn't eat properly. He would leave food hanging around the house and half of it would be gone because rodents love unattended food. I heard that on one visit, firemen had even seen a large rat dragging a small joint of meat across the bare wooden floorboards towards the basement. Three of the firefighters had screamed allegedly. I was approached by my manager because he felt that I was the most appropriate officer to take B on as a possible customer, where the local authority would fund my services directly to my employer. I had an idea it would be interesting short-term work, and I wasn't to be disappointed.

T was living in an illustrious looking 4-storey house a stone's throw from the centre of the city. The front door was sometimes left open, sometimes not. As you entered, you would notice the soiled flooring and the old carpets in a state of rapid deterioration. On the ground-floor, the front room contained an NHS bed and some old furniture pieces. It was where his mother spent her last days before she died of cancer. Across from there was his kitchen which was a remnant of the early seventies, barely usable and in severe decay. An ancient kettle and a sparking microwave on its last dangerous legs provided basic heating facilities. He told me how he had once trapped a rat below the sink, hearing it fight to escape until it had eventually died. Its brothers lived downstairs in the cellar and even caused alarm to the firemen. (I was talking to *T* one morning and a medium sized rodent scuttled past my feet and underneath his sofa. I shrieked moderately). In fairness the whole house was falling apart. Some of the rooms were carpeted but they were threadbare. The floorboards in many of the rooms were rotten and unsafe. You could see through the third-floor toilet down to the second-floor bathroom. The house had old wiring, ancient plumbing and heating which didn't work. The fire brigade had been called as had the police on several occasions, as he had been lighting fires within the boundaries of his house and often inside, because he had no working radiators. His home was a Grade 2 listed building, as were many of the buildings nearby, with proud and rude snobs for neighbours, who were adamant that he was not going to succeed in letting the tone down. Ironic, as he had lived there for far longer than anyone else had in that street. The police wanted to appease and keep the peace, the locals wanted him gone and somewhere in between, a little old man with not much in his hands except for a state pension and a minor gambling habit, was trying to live his life as best he could without interference. He could barely read at all but recognised some letter-shapes. The winter was coming fast. He needed help.

This was to be the finest example I had ever seen of multi-agency intervention. We had five reps from the local authority including a manager of environmental health, director of communities and her deputy, housing options manager, lead fire-fighter, police beat-sergeant, and to cap it all, the assistant manager of all the social workers in the city was on board. There were others too, including Ellie, a first-year social work student who shadowed me for a few months. It turned out that I had a pivotal part to play in the whole situation as it was housing and expediting a suitable solution that would save *T*. I brought as many strands together and tried to achieve all I could with GP intervention, staving off the courts and coordinating essential paperwork from the DWP. (I told Ellie that this case would be one of the best possible groundings for her studies.) It emerged that all along, he had been financially abused by a woman he knew and trusted. The lawyers weren't aware of that one. We were, and we managed to get on top of it, leading to a prosecution later on down the line. Where there's money, some people will take advantage and *T* being alone and isolated, was too trusting. Suffice to say, we were all on fire for a solution and it felt beyond good to be part of such a capable and willing team with so much influence and goodwill to work together. This was one of those rare moments in life where all the right ingredients came together into the pot at exactly the right time to safeguard an elderly man whose health was poor, his eyesight bad, his body decaying and his outlook mere survival.

Within about nine weeks of speedy collective intervention, we got him moved across town to a quaint sheltered bungalow with heating, hot water and cooking facilities. This worked out for a short time only, as he was taken advantage of by some men he knew and was almost arrested under suspicion of possessing 'bomb-making chemicals' which they had persuaded him to store at his place. As soon as his inheritance came through, he happily moved to a purpose-built retirement living flat with modern amenities in a beautiful semi-rural setting.

Poetic justice was to occur when he moved out of his original house. The lead social worker told me that no sooner than he had waved goodbye to his childhood home with the neighbours congratulating themselves for their small 'victory', than his brother moved in temporarily. His sibling liked nothing better than to messily 'repair' old cars in his forecourt, with a noise akin to a nuclear power-station. Meanwhile, *T* was self-contained and was well-away from the unsafe building, the accusations of the pompous and destructive couples next door...and rats.

In every street in every town, there is likely to be such a man who has been sidelined. We all need connection and we all need help from time to time...

A man without a mission

I first visited the house on a cold grey day and had been warned by my colleague that it was going to be heart-wrenching, as she carried in some spare clothes and toys for the young girl just home from school. We found the dad asleep on the sofa next to a 1L bottle of cheap *Lambrini*. He got himself together- which was upright- and as he talked I warmed to him because he seemed quite open and amiable. He had a deceased ex-partner, but the children were at risk, because simply put their dad was incapable of looking after himself, let alone two adolescent children. The eleven-year-old was a delightful girl who was simply not fed, clothed or guarded properly. The older boy was confused yet able. I only met him once. I was to realise that appearances can be deceptive, and there was so much professional intervention that Dad didn't really have to do much, as it was mostly taken care of, from grants and benefits to constant looking-in on the minors. He had even allowed several fifteen-year-olds high on weed into his house, crucially upstairs into a bedroom where his daughter slept. This next bit was the clincher for me that the guy had his own interests at heart and no one else's...

The main social worker and I exchanged numbers as it was going to be helpful for us to share key information and insights. I found out that a sizeable grant had been applied for, solely for the express purpose of buying furniture for the home. £800 had been spent - not on new beds, chairs or bedside tables - but exclusively on class-A drugs. He had admitted to jacking up in the downstairs loo behind a closed door, while only a few feet away his daughter was watching TV. I was to fill out a 6 month-review form of his present wellbeing and when it got to the section on finances, I asked him how it was going. He told me he had "been given a grant, but that it had all gone on bills...you know how it is...". I didn't even flinch and carried on writing, responding that I did "know exactly how it is". (He didn't know that I knew.)

At the second round-table professionals CIC *(Child in care)* meeting to which I had been invited, there were about twenty different reps from various agencies around the city meaning that this was an incredibly serious matter, and the second of three large scale meetings I was to attend. I felt like the least-knowledgeable and the least-able to participate, let alone come up with anything useful. How wrong I was. The Chair singled me out as someone she was clearly impressed by as I was willing to organize repairs, emergency locks and fencing to the home that day, making safer the vulnerable occupants. It was just my job. Each representative stated the facts and their professional concerns with care and clarity. Dad was not on trial, but he was called to account for his side of things by the Chair, who pulled no punches. I also noted a willingness at the conference for Dad to allow the kids to move in with their aunt in the next city, as a superior permanent solution on the proviso that her housing situation stabilized. Outside the doors, his mood changed, he became defiant; he retracted his statement and growled a low slur: it would never happen. He started to make a turn on me and became quite sly.

I had to abandon ship eventually, as there was more professional hovering over that house than a fleet of sightseeing helicopters over Niagara Falls. I felt unable to represent him without bias, so I bowed out. I don't think there was any love lost between myself and my former client. It had been leaked to me that he hated me, because I was in contact with his sister-in-law giving her general housing advice. I felt for him, even though he had been negligent of his duty of care as a father.

Here was a man who had certainly been left to fend for himself, with a history of being abandoned by those who were supposed to care for him in his formative years. Is it any wonder then that he was incapable of looking after anyone else?

Staring into space

I signed this gentleman up to our service with my manager, as he lay in his bed in his front room, whose window overlooked the main road with all the associated heavy traffic rolling by. *N* was a small man, friendly enough and appreciative of any input. He would listen and zone out but was surprisingly lucid and trusting. He had a diagnosis; bi-polarism. Nothing to be afraid of, but he had a kind of split personality apparently, though whenever I saw him, he seemed no trouble and no different at all from the last time. He had been forced to leave his highly unusual home because it was unsafe and unfit for habitation. It takes a lot for a local authority to serve a '*section 76 notice*' like this but serve it they did, and *N* was happy to take a ground floor flat just a half mile from the city centre. I spoke to the council officer who had issued the notice and the report and completely understood the reasons for it. To satisfy the recommendations, *N* would have had to have spent tens of thousands of pounds to improve and install heating and hot water systems, as well as address various structural problems with his building, before arranging to have it re-inspected. There was one other thing that was a little more disturbing about the building. No, it wasn't haunted. *N* told me how he had opened his small fridge one day and jumped back with alarm, as a large black rat was staring at him from the inside. Rats had gnawed their way through the back of the refrigerator as they had smelt food. I had it on good report that the whole domicile was riddled with them and for that reason alone, I suspected it was why he didn't seem in any hurry to return.

Here was a man who would often stare into space and act as though time was of no concern. He would lie in his bed and ponder things, listening to *Radio 4*, and absorbed by matters he might only share once in a while. His outlook was a mixture of positivity and inactivity. He had a small group of friends who would look in on him and keep in contact which was helpful for his mental health. Financially, he was in a position that many professionals would be proud of, as he had managed to save an enormous amount of benefits and other money through frugal living. I would occasionally have to dip into it with his approval, to pay off unforeseen bailiff bills or keep water supply connected to his old property, but other than that, he was very solvent if he needed to draw against funds. Occasionally he would show me old sepia photographs of his childhood years, and it was clear that he missed his parents, and the love of his life along the way. He had even invented a board game in his workshop which he desperately wanted to be trialled by adults and children. N had also been a focal character in his community, organising an annual party for all the locals. This had slipped away as he became less able to look after himself.

I lost touch with him for a couple of days, and despite my calls I couldn't get an answer. Although I only saw him usually once a week, I had a strong sense that I should pop in without delay. I found him laid on the floor caught between the bedroom and the kitchen. Having fallen and been unable to lift himself up, he had been there for two days, unable to alert anyone day or night. He had soiled himself and was very weak. The ambulance arrived within 10 minutes, the paramedics performed their observations and he was bundled off to hospital for various tests, an operation and a monitored recovery. He had suffered a kidney infection and was subsequently given a reablement personal care package and community nurse involvement. From then on, he was urged, with his consent, to pay for a pair of 'PAs' who could look after him on a twice-daily basis. My role became less-necessary, but I saw that my replacements weren't quite as savvy as I hoped with a lot of the paperwork side of things that I would take the lead on. I bowed out.

It's been about three years since I last saw him, but each time I happen to be driving past, I throw a casual glance towards his flat door and can see the windows open as normal, indicating he's still there, probably laid down thinking, staring into space and cloaked in a strange peace that belies his physical being. His listed building is still there, and to my knowledge remains in a state of slow decay. Just like its owner.

How many of us could while away the days pondering what we might have done, as the days escape into the ether of time?

PART TWO

Chapter Six

Illusions and aftershave

Illusions. If you've ever looked around you at the everyday world and thought that something's not quite right, almost as though everything has been *engineered*, then perhaps your eyes are starting to open. Adam Curtis, film-maker and director of '*Hypernormalisation*' (2016) summarises; "*We live in a fake world.*" Here's my take on the everyday world....

We the public have consciously given control over to politicians and financiers who have created this calming fake world for us in the west because behind the scenes would be too shocking and repulsive for us to contemplate let alone accept. Guess what? We have accepted the fake without asking too many questions, because it's easier. Give me the smartphone, broadband, wi-fi, *Sky*-package, *Amazon Prime*, *Netflix*, right to vote, credit cards, payment plan, holiday, *IKEA*, *Apple*, *Hollister*, *Superdry*, brands on the doorstep ad nauseam and I will become the willing consumer in this fake world. I will accept the news that is being streamed unto me and the conclusions that they want me to make. Millions like me will do the same and thereon is born popular public opinion, discussed and commented on in privacy and online.

If you've ever marvelled at a new store coming to town, when you pass the shop front and look inside, you'll see the bare brickwork, the plasterboard waiting to be put up, lights hanging down, electrics and plumbing visible- in short, a construction site. A few days prior to opening, you may catch a glimpse of the distinctive brand-panelling being drilled into the walls, covering what we always knew was there, with a comforting hi-tech durable plastic facade ready to welcome shoppers. Outside, the homeless man commands his pitch, shivering in a hoodie as he sits on a blanket with his eyes pleading, as the people walk past avoiding eye-contact. This is the world we have allowed and that we have no real control over. Phew, got that off my chest.

Smell. Such a basic sense that can take you back to a place, a person or a time. A perfume or an aftershave can take you somewhere in your heart, to a beautiful memory or an event you want to forget. *Eau de toilette, eau de parfum or cologne?* What we are sold on TV commercials is the promise of a something greater because we use this or that brand. Are you a *Sauvage, Lion* or just *Man*? These are some of the many advertising descriptions: *'victory in a bottle', 'the timeless gentleman'* and *'untouchable confidence'*. As classy as all these bottles may look, as much as they cost and as bold the promises made, it's all an illusion. Pour Homme. Illusion and aftershave: I'll tell you next what I think they have in common.

The smell of death

It was Rememberance Sunday parade day a couple of years ago when I chanced upon a middle-aged gentleman, in smart green uniform with a couple of medals on his lapel, as I walked with my family down a side street. I forget how we entered conversation, but I think it started with me saying, "You must have seen some terrible things in your time..." He replied that he "had seen some shocking things that stay with you for years after". He told me he was a bin-man but one of the hardest things that hit him was when he found a dead cat laying in between some rubbish bags. "I didn't touch it, but the smell got onto my clothes. It was the *smell*; it took me straight back to Bosnia when we had been digging and found those mass graves and the smell of dead bodies. You can never forget what you've seen. That cat triggered it for me...the smell of death and I just burst into tears..."

Illusion, mental health and identity

This chapter, I'll admit, probably sits at odds with all the rest, but I *have* to write it, because as awkwardly as it may at first appear, illusion is directly related to mental health and identity in more ways than I first thought. For example, if I believe my identity comes from what I wear, my haircut, where I live or from what I do during my daytimes, then that false identity must have come from somewhere external. These things are transient, momentary and superficial. You don't tend to see careers, favourite clothing brands, vehicles or hairstyles referred to on gravestones. Then why is it that we place such emphasis on them in the here and now? I've done this myself too. In my younger days, I would only venture out if I was wearing a particular make of t-shirt, jacket or jeans, realising eventually that the branding guys were having the last laugh by using the slogan *'For successful living'*. It sold a dream, a quest, a fantasy and I bought into it. (But I did feel good.)

A false narrative tries to lead us all into believing that 'this is it'; we are hemmed in to one particular pathway as the illusion gives us enough rein to create a life of *just enough* comfort, money or 'success'. The land of 'just enough'. It almost seems wrong to desire *more* than just enough. I often live in this zone, but I always wonder about what could happen if I aimed higher than the achievable. I'm not talking about money only, but also about personal goals, achievements and ambitions. These could be studying, helping others, raising a family (including another's), starting a charity, highlighting a cause, standing up for an injustice, tackling discrimination, exposing a lie, befriending the friendless or simply beautifying a run-down area. One thing that most of the men I supported in my work life as illustrated in Part One had in common was this: they had not the ability or wish to look after anyone else but themselves. You can see the link between 'just enough' and selfishness. It's something I battle with myself every day.

I once did a blind-test with an aftershave twenty years back with a few people I worked with. They all liked it and plumped for the expensive brands: *'Calvin Klein'*, *'Tommy'* or *'Davidoff'*. I had the last laugh: *"Wrong! Superdrug, Forest Fresh, £1.99."* Guess what? It's so popular they're still making it. Time to get serious....

Wanted: Looking down the barrel of a gun

Sofiwan our driver had parked up his Hyundai Accent in a layby outside a fast food restaurant in *Mansour,* a district of Baghdad. The American military had taken control of the capital and most of the main towns while the hunt for a dictator was on. *Operation Iraqi Freedom* now followed the first operation *Desert Storm* twelve years later. The July air was sweltering, and the car was baking with six of us crammed into a car meant for five. I appeared to be the only one who noticed but there was an American armoured vehicle right behind us, manned by two soldiers, one of whom was signaling furiously from his turret at *Sofiwan* who appeared to be totally ignoring him. He had an assault rifle pointing at the car the whole time. After the longest two minutes with the engine running, we opened the doors at Mikey's suggestion we go get some food, and as I exited the passenger door, I looked up, holding my hands in the air instinctively. I was looking down the barrel of an M16A4 trained on *me* only, as the sweat poured down the small of my back. I was hardly a wanted man, but the soldier's focus never left me until I waved, and we headed down the path to the local takeaway. It's a moment I'll always remember but I never felt afraid, just ready for friendly fire. A euphemism for 'we mistook you for the enemy.' (Me? I was more like an unfit, clean-shaven Joe Wicks.)

Allure: The Trophy wife

One of my legal practice course colleagues *J*, came from a beautiful Caribbean island, via another continent, was older than most there, and had an army background. You could tell he was a tough guy, behind his amiable exterior. He opened up to me one day, as he smoked his way through what was going on for him in his love life. As we stood together talking outside the city centre's university building with traffic whizzing by in the spring air, he showed me a picture on his phone of his latest girlfriend. I could see why his heart was torn between study and play. My friend had met an Eastern European girl who obviously paid great attention to every last detail of her looks and was using her best assets to attract wealthy men who could keep her in Middle Eastern luxury. (Some might call it prostitution. I call it overuse of foundation, blush and lip-gloss.) He would travel over to Dubai as often as he could to stay, but his student funds were depleting. He knew he had to study but he was captivated, and as he expanded on this, he revealed he had an 'addiction' to dolly-birds like this. In truth, it probably fed his ego as much as it did hers, and we both knew that it would end up in hurt for him. She had indicated to him there were others needing her affections. J was being played and had answered his own questions himself as we spoke with the world going by. She would not end up being his trophy wife of course, as our mums would warn us about girls like this when we were boys. He would do better to concentrate on his studies, gain his qualification and run. Far, far away. The trophy wife was an illusion.

How can the ego demand so much but the trinkets we think are so valuable can actually destroy us inside?

Obsessed: The fantasy holds power

I knew a man who lived a couple of miles away with his wife and two young boys, and all seemed well enough. Nice house, nice family, good job. That was the veneer. What lay beneath was more troubling. He was host to an invisible parasite that I could only describe now, as not a small insect, but more like an ugly man-size wasp, claws fused into his back over years. He would carry the weight of this demon everywhere as it controlled his thoughts and his actions night and day. Its smug power had been made complete by first giving its prey a little peek that had become a mild curiosity, then a fixation and finally a dependency. From the first night of his marriage, it became clear to his wife that she was not what he desired. He was hooked by a fantasy which even caused him to lose a succession of jobs. He would go into town he admitted, to take photos of females as they walked around. His addiction would cause him to stare at a computer screen for hours during the night, taking in the illusion of pleasure, while his real love lay sleeping in their bed, resigned to taking second place. The wasp eventually won, as the couple broke up within a decade, and their sons were left wondering why daddy could only see them on alternate weekends. He had been completely controlled and broken by an illusion. The hold is so strong for so many men.

Why couldn't he fight it and win? All he needed to do was twist the sword into that belly and free himself.

Only the Brave: fighting the voices

I had hit a juncture in my early thirties. Nothing I did seemed to be working and I sensed it was time to press 'reset'. I didn't want to, but something inside told me that although it was going to be painful, I would have to do it, like a gardener pruning his favourite rosebush; cutting it back to make it even more fruitful. I had already handed in my notice at the restaurant I had worked at for ten years. I was feeling out of control like baby-Moses in his basket in the river, being swept away by the currents.

I was to see my sister and brother-in-law who live on a Greek island to get some focus and off-season solitude. The morning before the day of my flight, I was just leaving the house, when the postie delivered a package through the letterbox. I opened it and found it was a book from one of my friends whom I don't see very often. (The last time we had met, we were in Baghdad, Iraq.) I flew out to Greece the following day, feeling melancholy and whilst over there, managed to get my ticket extended, impossibly, for a further two weeks with no charge. I read that book a total of three times over my stay on the island, and realised how it wasn't by chance that I had still been at home to receive it. I was *meant* to take it with me. That book revolutionised the way I looked at myself, my heart and my place in the world.

On my return, I quickly carried out a sequence of painful yet necessary things. I split with my band of four years, with whom I had desperately tried to 'make it' and had tied many hopes upon. Just as painful, I also called it a day with my then-girlfriend; I reasoned there was nothing wrong with either of us, but 'the combination of us' wasn't working. I moved out of my best friend's house where I had been living for five joyous years and returned to take up my old room at the folks' place. My work-life was now dependent on agency-assignments. I was now at rock-bottom mentally, trying to make sense of what I had just done and wondering if I had truly lost it. I sat on my bed in the quiet one late afternoon that summer, hanging my head when I heard the taunting whisper: *"Look at you now, and look at what you've done...you're just a miserable failure who'll never get anything right...."* I almost agreed. With all my resolve I fought back in my head with a determination that belied my lowly state. I've come to comprehend the nature of those whispers. Anything that seeks to devalue, degrade or even destroy you is not from the One who cares for you. Voices, I'm still here and still up for a fight. (I knew two people personally who experienced voices, and they were as real to them as you talking to me. I heard one of them arguing back with a silent agitator. A real argument, not fake, but I just couldn't hear the other side. It was disturbing.)

Boss: Illusion in the workplace

Talking of fights, have you ever been bullied at work? I have, by two bosses who may/ may not have been aware of what they were doing. One definitely was. I dreaded daily the act of going into work, feeling the stress rise up as I neared the gates. I was the assistant manager for a site under a manageress. That person would go behind my back to check with junior colleagues that I had done things properly, would regularly try to belittle and criticise me in front of other managers or visitors and change the goalposts of once-agreed parameters. I stood my ground, yet with forced-respect and a sense that although I could not change anything, this would one day work out for my good. I left that job after about 20 months, with only half of my team signing my leaving card. (I should have known something was not right just at the point I was joining the team, when she announced there was no space for me on their table at the staff Christmas meal and told me to find another one in front of everyone.) I was to find out years later that despite her territorial nature, she had been forced to depart. Her employers had found fault with her and she was dismissed. The unimaginable had happened.

The other boss? Well, that person was aggressive and crushing, yet could be quite personable. Ex-army officer. He described himself as too much of a maverick for them and that was why he left the armed forces. I had been on eggshells in his presence for months, as like a grenade, you never knew when he was going to blow. I even heard him say that he lived his life on certain principals which I truthfully saw very little evidence of. One morning I deliberately took my time in getting myself ready, which was very out of character, but I was at near-breaking point over the weekend, and knew I had to rise up and make a stand. He phoned me as I was shaving and chirpily asked where I was. I explained I would not be coming in (to stand on parade) until he understood that the way he would speak to me was completely unacceptable, and before stepping into work, I would need to talk. (I had timed my action deliberately as without me there, two paid jobs would have to be cancelled.) We spoke briefly, but sadly it was turned all back on me. Needless to say, it wasn't ever going to change anything, except for one key element: I had stood up for myself and was no longer a push-around. I lasted a few more weeks before being honourably discharged.

In both cases, I am sure they could justify their actions to themselves, but the common factor was that during conversations about their past experiences, they opened up that they had been treated badly themselves. That had caused them to carry a protective shell which involved craftily or openly attacking as a *defence*. Looking back and writing this now, I can see how *utterly broken* they must have been, to pour out their poison, bitterness and wrath on others around them, their subordinates. The twist was that it gave me the qualities of endurance, perseverance and resilience. I would need those qualities for things ahead, yet I did not understand it at the time. As I looked around me, I saw that the longer workers endure a bullying persona, the more normalised it becomes, to the extent it becomes tolerated, accepted and near-impossible to call out. We all bring our faults, judgements and prejudices into the workplace with us, however much we disguise it with corporate veils of harmony and acceptance. The illusion of one happy work-family can be snapped in half incredibly quickly by conflict, bullying or shaming. If only we could admit that we are all broken, but that would be a step too far for so many of us men, as to admit vulnerability is too often seen as a weakness.

In nearly every workplace I have been employed, there is often, but not always, an unfair boss or leader, a manipulative or sly individual, an outspoken person who doesn't really think before they speak, a slacker, an outsider, a critic and a gossip. It would have to be a very bad day indeed for all of these characteristics to be wrapped up into one personality, yet it happens. (Sometimes, I have been many of the above to my shame.) Conversely, a high performing team could have all of these character weaknesses embodied into a bunch of grafters who are actually an excellent complement. Most of the time we are good at disguising ourselves. Maybe you can see parallels in workplace scenarios of your own? One friend of mine had but uncovered a wasps' nest of envy and hate. Here's his story...

Mercedes Benz Man Private: Tribunal time

Being someone who usually thrives in the company of positive people combined with a working knowledge and love of prestige cars, meant that *D* ought to have had a long career in the automotive sales industry. When I knocked around with him years ago, I could see that he was a natural and gifted team player with a strong customer service ethos. (I must stop sounding like I'm trapped in a CV.) Here's the essence of what he said:

"Where to begin? OK... The motor trade has been and always will be a snake pit of toxicity. The issue is incompetent narcissistic-sociopathic-ego-maniac-management and after jumping around five brands, I can confirm this as factual, within a 90 percent average. My experiences exacerbated my mental health which I've suffered with for many years and on medication for stress/anxiety and depression. The motor trade is full of ego, this much is true, and I can be guilty of it myself, however, to scapegoat a person within a mob mentality due to jealousy is something I could never do. At the expense of blowing my own trumpet, I was generally the top salesman in my field; this created a lot of resentment from fellow colleagues which I believe was the catalyst for my victimisation. There are far too many examples to mention but I've suffered gaslighting from them moving my keys around on the keyboard ever so subtly, moving the 'I' and 'O' which created issues when trying to unlock your system when customer facing, to the point the customer leaves and you are left stressed and confused, calling IT to change password which still doesn't work! Then comes the passive aggression, rooms stop talking when you enter, then laughter and comments behind your back that you know about but can't prove. I believe managers create cultures and one example would be a compulsive, lying, wide-boy manager who has a 'god-complex' who feels threatened by you because of your skillset size and general confidence. I refer to it as 'small man syndrome', some unprofessional 'managers' feel threatened by anything that they are insecure about whether that's down to height build or even confidence. I was pushed out of one company due to raising bullying grievances and whistle-blowing on a serious breach of Covid health and safety. I went off sick with depression due to the vile toxic environment I found myself in, I was in a very low place, feeling helpless, asking myself why I was not supported by any of the immature and unprofessional management that were somehow promoted to these roles? I even suffered verbal abuse; one particular manager swore at me in front of colleagues, but the colleagues denied this happened. My company phone usually went missing from time to time which meant I would miss out on the hunt group sales calls. Management just thought this was hilarious, to give you an insight. Again, I could write a book! But that's your job and maybe one day we could work together? Anyway, how this made me feel... I felt bullied and deflated and for a 6ft 17 stone man this was hard to comprehend, bullied by cowardly snakes who thrived on triggering me. I forgot to mention, due to previous problems at another dealership, I decided to brave up and declare my mental health condition in order to receive some support and maybe reasonable adjustments if need be. Instead it was used against me. The reality (not that I'm violent and have no criminal record, just to mention) is that I could have snapped said-people like toothpicks but of course, this would've gotten me into a world of trouble, and they all knew it. For them it was fun to bully someone a lot bigger and more confident, (perhaps this is my ego talking now,) but in my experience, the less aesthetically attractive people tend to hate others who may look different to them... I'm comfortable saying this based on this individual's lack of morals and integrity... he's a vile human being in my opinion."

As I write this, I am dismayed, because dear reader, my feeling is that on the balance of probabilities, you may well have suffered bullying like this, even if you have been able to contain it. *D* is not playing the victim and he's taking on the system. (I've offered my services if he needs a pretend-lawyer, but he winced when I asked him if he was going to take it to a 'Terry-Tribunal', and said he'd prefer to do a couple of beers. I don't think I was cut out to be a Larry-Lawyer...)

Exit: interviewed alone

About fifteen years ago, I lasted just three months into one job and I left within the probation period as another opening became available. It was a strange clinical place with obvious fragmentation, and I could not click with anyone there except for a couple of characters. I sensed that people didn't truly want to be there. The middle-aged woman in charge had a touch of glamour about her as she paraded about the place. She was given a local TV interview and made great show of this as she obviously liked the attention. Knowing I was to be married within a short space of time, she kept making remarks like *'You'll see...'*, sighing with mock heaviness and giving her opinion of my marriage before it had even begun, based on her failures. It appeared her second one wasn't all that she had hoped it would be either. She once pushed my back to nudge me forward to help someone of importance which irritated me. I watched her behaviours carefully and realised that her work was her life. I was invited to an 'exit interview'. There was no-one else in the room, so I filled in the 'interview' form myself, not pulling any punches about the working atmosphere and culture there. I finalized it in capital letters across the front page: 'INTERVIEW CONDUCTED BY MYSELF.' She couldn't even make time to attend. I was contacted by another more senior employee weeks later who asked me if I would support his grievance against her too. I wasn't the only one then.

Above the law: Burnout syndrome

Someone I know is an HR Director for a huge utilities company. He asked me how my law-career was going. When I replied that it was effectively not going as none of my many applications even for paralegal work were working, this was his view: "Simon, I think you've had a lucky escape. From what I've seen with many lawyers, is their firms overload them and burn them out!" I was to find out that behind the self-assuredness oozing through staff photos on websites of the many law firms I wasted time on researching, is a culture of clock-watching and intensive pressure to charge clients the maximum, while smiling and shaking hands. It is common for partners to concentrate on bringing in new business and retaining fee payers, while those below effectively do the donkey work. Mental health of barristers and solicitors is not exactly at an all-time high, judging by my further research. It's not just the self-employment side, the retention of facts or the pressure on the brain to come up with convincing legal arguments, but also the feeling of being swamped by others' problems and the feeling of responsibility coupled to the pressure to be in control of solutions. (To a similar degree, I felt much of this in my advocacy work.)

Icon: The professional mask

Doctors, accountants, lawyers. Directors, CEO's and financiers. Captains, generals and admirals. There's a lot of kudos wrapped up in those job-titles. How much respect is afforded to those who hold those qualifications and roles. Rightly so, as they indicate the slog that men wade through, and the lengths that people will go to, to achieve these aspirations, and they are vital positions. I think you know where I may be heading.... Have you ever come across a man whose position is his *life?* I think you understand me. I've met a few of this kind. His whole persona is cool, calm and collected, demeanour is in-control, coming across as sophisticated and having *everything*. He smells no more forceful than a bottle of *CK One*. Real life happens to everyone, with its dirt, its disappointment and its drudgery. It doesn't smell so good. Mask-wearing must be like 'imposter syndrome'. Incredibly emotionally draining, watching your back for *Brutus* the whole time, and worst of all, lonely. Jobs come and jobs go. I think the hardest thing is to keep yourself balanced, recognising that when all is said and done, no matter how important your career might be, it can easily shift, according to so many variables including the economy, demand and even more importantly your health and personal circumstances. (I write this understanding the present times of course.) The professional mask is an appealing one for so many men because the pro-sheen with its superficial finish deflects attention from deeper issues. The mask acts out its role to deter anything that would threaten its theatre. It denies access to any unwanted intrusion and won't give anyone a backstage pass to the dressing room.

Denim Illusion: what we want others to see...

We all portray what we want others to see, and we are all capable of wearing masks. What do masks do? They disguise us. They give us a different character. They tell a different story from reality. They entertain others. To some extent, we all wear them, willingly or unwittingly, because convention tells us we have to act in a certain way, or we have to present only the good parts or the worthwhile parts of our lives to others. Brokenness is seen as weakness. Strength is evident in a soaring scale of material worth and influence. What an unbelievable pressure that presents to us men- the breadwinners, the providers and the ones who are supposed to keep it together.

I know a few men who have to wear the professional mask but actually, they are as real as the builders swearing at each other on the roof next door. They hold positions like 'Vice-President' of a bank, 'MRICS Chartered Surveyor', 'ICT Director', 'Professor', 'Executive and Business Leader' and 'Land Developer'. They like their coffee strong, restoring vintage *Vespas* and *Gretsch White Falcons*, competing in triathlons, driving battered *Land Rovers* across muddy fields and watching rock bands. They have come to understand that real life involves changing soiled nappies, re-mortgaging, worrying about their children, business failure, divorce and death. They'll happily admit: "The more I know, the less I understand..." (Actually, that's my line.) My vice-president banker friend found himself in a festival beer tent one night, crammed with men who suddenly spontaneously burst into hymns just like at a rugby match but with more vigour. It sounded like the most spiritual experience of his life, as I imagined volume, smiles and real ale in hands. I bet the angels were hanging off the rafters joining in too.

James Bond 007: A matter of national security?

Following my vocational course in Legal Practice, I felt ceilings start to lift off me as I started to realise that all that was stopping me, was *me*. Not wanting to be restricted to lawyerdom, and true to my base impulses of trying new things, I thought I would go for MI5. The security service had been advertising nationally so I went for a trio of roles, just for a laugh. After being successful at the first three stages for 'Intelligence Officer Development Programme', I ended up being invited to a selection centre for Stage Four, in central London for a 9am start. I left the house at 3.30am and by 04.30, I was on a coach bound for the capital. Arriving at the building with just 10 minutes to spare, I checked in and waited. All around me were younger candidates, in smart business attire like myself. But it was the tension in the room I won't forget. It was like the guys there fancied themselves as either Sean, Daniel or Pierce. The girls? Not so much choice, as it was either Moneypenny, M or one of the double agents. Everyone seemed to be waiting for a bomb to go off, or to be announced as the winner of the *'I most look like an undercover agent'* award. As I absorbed my surroundings, I saw an empty *Walkers Ready Salted* packet on the nearby table. It took all my powers of resistance to stop myself from reaching out for it, blowing into it and popping it, screaming; "Get down!!" This may explain why I eventually failed this stage. I didn't actually have to say anything, as it was probably written all over my face. I also missed out what was to be a crucial fact in a report I wrote as part of the test: a set of surveillance recommendations on characters in the brief. Coming home that afternoon, I considered that if I was to be offered the next stages and beyond, the pay scale would not sustain me and my family in any way. On a greater level, I wondered about my wholesale belief in the government and if I could justify to myself potentially being part of an organisation which uses covert operations, illegal surveillance methods and torture. Well *maybe*, but only if I got a new suit, an Aston and a 75ml bottle of James Bond Quantum, then I too could be 'bold, daring and masculine. Whether you're suited & booted or relaxing in the sun - this is the perfect scent for any confident male.' What an illusion. Even with Top Notes of Bergamot and Juniper Berries....

Legend: Worldly to wise

I have a friend I hardly see anymore as our lives are quite different, but I do try to check in with him once in a blue moon. He is what I would call a 'career policeman' who has climbed up the ranks into 'detective chief inspector' and beyond into the realms of SIO (senior investigating officer) and even higher, as the lead on various high-profile cases of national importance. One such case he had heavy involvement in was an investigation into a children's home and cover up of long-term child abuse. He would spend most of his working weeks away from home, returning at weekends to see his family. His work demands much, and he gives much in return. I think he struggles internally with the push-pull and I casually observe that his role has given him much of his worldly identity. He keeps himself in good shape and is a rugged handsome chap. Beyond that, my friend shared with me a few years back a dream he had about being on a desert island. All the younger men were procreating with the beautiful girls, but he was sitting on a rock wondering why he was left out. He was told he now had *wisdom*. I don't need to fill in his response. The dream was allegorical. Maybe his head was trying to reconcile the passage of time with the passing of youth and into advanced middle age. Women use *Oil of Olay* to delay the outward passage of time, but what do us men get? *Men's Anti-ageing moisturiser*. Failing that it's *Brut and Old Spice*. There's nothing else on the shelf that can help with the passing of youth which my friend laments (not even from *Superdrug*), so we had better embrace wisdom. I think I can still hear him crying now....

Guilty: Order in the court

While in the mid throes of studying for my law degree, I would occasionally pop down to my local magistrates' court to observe cases. I used to see men and women standing outside and it was interesting to see the social sciences at work. I would notice young men in ill-fitting suits, offset sometimes by trainers to give a serious/casual impression. It would be obvious who the defendants were most of the time. You just looked at them and unfortunately judged them by their appearance. Guilty before they'd even stubbed out their butt ends and gone through the body scanners on the ground floor. I sat in at the back on various cases, observing and keeping quiet. One was of a woman whose relationship had ended, and having fallen apart, was caught drunk at the wheel of her motionless car. She had a good brief who cited her 'usual good character' explaining this was a one-off slip. She was let off with cautions and community service. Another case saw the defendant unremorseful for a civil affray, with the main JP ordering him several times to take his hands out of his pockets. Yet more cases involved breaches of tenancies, repayment plans for outstanding bills, claims for damages or lost earnings. Sometimes the 'respectable businessmen' were ruled against, because they had acted unjustly. The private family law cases were held behind doors closed to the public. The reminder was that these issues could happen to any of us. The illusion is that 'good people never get into trouble'.

Arabian Desert: Illusion in the everyday world

I'll admit that I love a good 'conspiracy theory'. The word theory implies that it is unsubstantiated. Often, when I delve a little deeper and find that these 'theories' tie in with research from various sources around the world, then I start to realise that there could be more truth in them than I dared realise. There is an 'alternative world' which The Matrix referred to: accessed by either 'the red pill or the blue pill'. I live in the world, but I take a strong interest in alternative explanations, immersing myself from time to time, coming up for air frequently. Then I have to back off a little to keep my sanity, as the exposure of the grand illusion is almost too great, that it threatens to destabilise what I know of as 'normal'. My own mental health has itself become imbalanced when I have immersed myself for too long in this 'alternative world'. From the Arabian deserts through to the built-up skyscrapers, something does not seem to stack up with the world outside. Fake world again?

It is vital that we keep a healthy awareness then, of events coming through our screens, but also to realise sadly, that we ought to filter 'news' as it is not always the truth. There is so much subliminal text in everything that comes through our screens and into our psyches. It reminds me of an episode of *Columbo*. Subliminal messaging is also a part of popular entertainment; everyone from *JayZ* to *Taylor Swift*. I have questioned why those weird shapes appear in videos by *Bruno Mars*, why *Lady Gaga's* performances are so artistically dark, and why some have apparently lamented how they sold their souls to get where they are? Really?! Yes, these things might actually happen even in our so called 'modern world'. Years ago, Paul Hewson and his band toured the world following their first crossover dance beats/ rock guitars album. Was it just harmless slogans they put up on the screen or did it mean something when the one came up, *'Everything you know is wrong'*? Like a lot of art, it points to the hidden made visible for a split second.

I've spent time going down the rabbit hole trying to find 'truth' and it has drawn me into side tunnels, I'll be honest. I now look at the world completely differently. With so many unsolved 'mysteries', you'll have to search a little harder, but you'll start piecing together a seemingly far-fetched, yet compelling picture. If like me, you find yourself quizzing the official details then zooming back out you may well follow it through perhaps to an alternative conclusion: *Illusion. How much more news could be faked? Dare I trust anything else I see or hear? It strikes me that we live in a world of illusion, where what seems to be real is probably not.*

This is gargantuan. I know so very little but think I'm well-informed, by recycling the news at work, at get-togethers, with friends and out in the world. If I were to stop and quiz the news, to actively filter it, I would do myself a real favour and take a step towards reality. (An iPhone equipped with a dozen apps in my children's hands does not make them sophisticated, similarly with me. Sometimes it's all I can do to turn the thing on....) Next time someone moans about politics generally and is convinced one party is better than the other *"because..."*, I challenge you to recall this piece of my writing about illusion. Have you ever considered why one party getting into power doesn't change things as radically as they originally promised? Could it be that the parties are not actually the ones pulling the strings? I'm not the only one who thinks there is a devious plan at work and it's global. Please do the research and draw your own conclusions; I have. There may well be more truth in these apparently subversive videos posted on *YouTube* than we would like to admit. (I watch them before they're taken down.) But do remember to keep breathing....(For the record, airliners are extremely powerful but carry a flimsy metal skin; a couple of seagulls flying into an engine, aka *bird-strike,* can bring a jet liner down, and there is plenty of everyday footage showing airport trucks accidentally colliding with airliners at just 20mph, completely writing them off. Airliners do go missing but do the maths and it's quite possible they ended up in military hangars. There is a shadow side. You knew it all along, didn't you?)

Illusione: What is real?

'What is real?' Is it the advert on TV promising that a certain low-fat cereal will guarantee you a flat stomach like the model who dives flawlessly into a waiting swimming pool? Is it the funeral payment plan endorsed by that nice, elderly man on TV, you know, the one you can trust because you can get a free pen and a gift voucher? Is it the pictures of the war in that hot Middle Eastern country where excitable local crowds are cheering when the statue of their despot gets pulled down, while American soldiers watch silently through their *Oakleys*? Are the adverts for well-known institutions with horses running by the ocean going to convince us that everything will be stable because they've been in business for longer than a century? We know that these are the creations of advertising agencies, selling us a dream, a veneer of something that provides us comfort and reassurance. That illusion should keep us in check for years, until crisis-time, when the realisation hits us that it was trickery all along.

XS: The Thorn-bird

It's now well known that there are a handful of programmers in Silicon Valley, California working on how they can make the next smartphones and hi-tech gadgets even more compulsive and addictive to users. *Give us excess of it that the appetite may sicken and so die.* And us? We are still so willing to embrace it all:- not just the technology but the whole package, and a little like the mythical 'thorn bird'*, we one day may sing the most beautiful song as we find the perfect thorn (technology) and impale ourselves on it. (*Celtic legend).

Impact: obeying the prompt...

Now I might be on my own here but stay with me. Every now and then I feel a prompt so tiny that I question whether I felt it or not. If it keeps coming back like a pin prick at my conscience, I'll listen. It's often while I'm doing something normal like tidying, working or walking through town. On this occasion it was the latter. Someone came into my head and he wouldn't go away. I went to buy him a cheap box of *Maltesers*, with the aim of popping into his small shop where he fixed phones and laptops, just to say "Hi" and to thank him for some recent successful repairs. His eyes lit up when I greeted him, and he was genuinely touched when I told him it was just a small gift to say thanks for the iPad fix. I asked him how he was doing and there was the opening. (I can always tell when someone's not OK. It's most of the time if we're honest. OK means "I have a pulse.") In the space of an almost unbroken 45 minutes, he revealed that he had a fractious relationship with his mum and brother, had just split with his long-term girlfriend and was going to move away to start over again. No mention of his dad. What we spoke about wasn't the key here. It's about the space and trust between two men who open up and actually talk about deeper things. He told me that when he sees me with my family, I looked like I've got it all together and can't have any problems. (You see, I'm right about illusion aren't I? The illusion of what someone sees, how well we disguise our problems and inner pain and give others what we want them to see.)

He even told me that he had talked to a friend about wanting to go to church to see if he could find God, whoever He might be. Before I left, I asked if I could pray with him before we were interrupted by customers. We gave each other a hug; this was in the days when you could do such a thing without fear of transmitting or receiving a virus. Funny that something so simple as a little red box of chocs can lead you into a space where someone feels they can trust you. I left him to it and that's the last time I saw him, a few years ago. I hope he finds real peace. You'll never know the impact you can have on another soul. *Samsung* to salvation.

Eternity: Belief

"Seek and thou shalt find...": you may well find what you're looking for... Can a belief in God or a 'religious' outlook help, or hinder a man whose mental health is not so stable, or who is confused about his identity? Hereon, I consider how belief may influence wellbeing...

Years ago, when I worked as a waiter in a restaurant, in the mid-afternoon between shifts I would sometimes wander across the road to a beautiful Catholic church. Before pushing open the heavy arched wooden door, I would often stay in the porch area and take in the words of *'The Desiderata'*, a most beautifully written piece which calls to our hearts. The Latin simply translates as *'things that are desired'* and the writer manages to write something which unifies every man and woman without dogma or force. Its beauty is universal. Having read the words and taken them in, I would venture into the quiet sanctuary, the door creaking behind me, in the hope that the church was empty of others. I would sit, usually on a pew somewhere near the back and remain still sometimes for up to a couple of hours. I would often kneel down, my head resting on my folded hands, focusing on the candlelight ahead, sometimes even falling asleep. *Cast your cares...My burden is light.* In the stillness of the building, even if there were others around, I felt less burdened, and enveloped by calm. My life was a constant race and these moments were like a saving grace, a chance to realign, to tune into the peace of God and to process who I was and what might lay before me. When I look back, I realise that it's in those moments I really started to find myself, by pausing, contemplating and meditating for a while. It didn't have to be a church. I had other favourite spots such as particular farm gates overlooking fields, benches near canals at dawn, level crossings and even an airport perimeter road beneath the starry skies. There was something comforting about being alone on a winter's evening with the galaxy above, whilst listening to a radio programme about missionaries in Albania, with colourful runway lights illuminating the darkness of an unusually quiet airfield.

That sense of being alone, yet *not really* being alone at all, has always remained in me. I like to think He's near me everywhere I go. Over the years I have read and personally experienced so much that has convinced me of the reality of God, that nothing could shift me now. I'm up for eternity. It doesn't mean that I have never faced dark, low or near-impossible times. Even though demons have beckoned me to follow them to destruction, I know that at least for me, there is a fight for my soul. My reason for being, my purpose and even my destiny is walked out daily. That means that in the practical every day *'Ordinary World'* as *Duran Duran* sang about, it's worked out in my motives, my heart's ambitions and the way I treat others, especially those who live closest to me. For men who feel like prisoners, I feel like inviting you to try looking for and finding the same peace that I find so liberating. You're not alone. You're really not.

Sauvage: Abuse of power in churches

It's unfortunate that pastors and vicars can sometimes abuse their power, and churches can sometimes become cult-like. I would estimate there's usually one borderline cult per town complete with associated victims. Does this mean we should throw the baby out with the bathwater? No, but act carefully, and if you're caught in the crossfire (ahem), try to remain balanced. We were caught up in a situation like this for several years. There was a lack of accountability, a culture of espionage and a recruitment programme of younger people to leadership positions.

Formerly it was a truly great place to belong to. My two friends 'Vice president' and 'ICT Director' listened to my moans. VP hinted at the church's professed name and drew this analogy, "Remember, countries with *democratic* in their title rarely are!" ICT Director paused and said, "Why don't you just tell them to 'F*** off?!'" I remember breathing somewhat lighter at that point knowing that I could pull that out of the bag if I ever needed to. As it happened, we eventually just left quietly by email. No hard feelings, no regret, just a feeling of learning a lesson. Halleluiah.

Euphoria: Miracle at the cashpoint

It was a cold wintry November afternoon as I entered the main branch of my bank off the high street and headed towards the machines ready to deposit my last few banknotes to keep my overdraft within its limit. I could not have felt lower. I had tried online in my usual way to see if I could have a loan approved but no joy. I had tried again by altering figures, but the algorithm got wise to my attempts. Then I tried to speak to a loan manager by phone but was turned down. I was getting desperate and depressed. The black horse was not interested in my sugar lumps. So much for trying to improve your employment options with a postgraduate diploma in law. I had made a handful of phone-calls in the weeks preceding, to determine whether or not I could apply for an 'IVA' (Individual voluntary arrangement or insolvency arrangement). It all felt wrong, but I also felt backed into a corner where I had borrowed so much just to afford life and complete the legal course, yet now could not afford the credit card repayments. If I took this route, this arrangement would probably affect job applications and my credit score, and I was going to have to put our house up as collateral. I was desperate. Money does that to you. I was stuck and the quicksand was taking me down fast. As I drew near to the deposit machine, I glanced over to the customer service desk and saw *A*, a branch manager. It was then that the still small voice I know spoke clearly to my heart: *"Talk to A."* ('I can't. I've already been turned down.') Again, the voice spoke softly: *"Talk to A."* ('I will, but only if there's no queue, once I'm done here.')

I paid in the notes and retrieved my card. There was no queue, so I walked straight over to him. A looked horrified once I explained the situation. *"I'm sure there's something we can do, Mr. Marton. I'll just see if one of my colleagues can fit you in......hold on a second... Great, Nicky's just had a cancellation and she can see you right now if you have the time!"* I made the time. A window in time.

Forty minutes later, I walked out of the bank with a loan to cover everything including ongoing affordable payments which would clear my recent student debts. No need to declare myself bankrupt. I was shouting: *'Thank you! Thank you! Thank you!'* in my heart to the One who has often made His still small voice clear to a deaf guy like me. I still feel that same relief, even now as I write this. A small pebble to many, that felt like a massive miracle to me. I looked back as I left the bank. I swear the black horse was smiling.

Straight to Heaven: if he made the choice

I knew a couple in their late fifties/ early sixties who were regular visitors to the restaurant. Table nine on a Friday night: R would always have one drink as she was driving, while N would always have a medium/ rare rump steak and get through a litre of house red. They ran a popular gym over the road, and we became good friends over the years. He would size my physique up, saying he could do something with it. (I bet he said that to all the bodybuilders.) He was a short man, full of good humour and army stories from his service days in Aden. His wife would roll her eyes at much of what he said. He had trained with Schwarzenegger and Lou Ferrigno among others and was quite possibly the strongest man I knew, but no-one dared mention *steroids*. He used to love reciting this line after a few brandies: *'Vive la mort, vive la guerre, vive le sacre mercenaire!'* He would often steer the conversation onto God, the devil, and how he would have to be let in through the gates of heaven as he hadn't been a bad bloke and He should understand. It was like his perception of God was as a colour sergeant-major, throwing people a nod to get in, just like climbing into the back of a Bedford MJ truck. I would try to explain who Jesus actually is in relation to the God-head, but he couldn't quite get past a guy who was sadly so often ineffectively portrayed with a blonde bouffant and a nightie. He said I was the only person he could talk to about God. (I can think of better-qualified persons.)

One day I discovered quite suddenly that he had been taken ill as he was not at his work Christmas lunch. He was in hospital and that's all I was told. Here's the sequence of events: I drove up the next afternoon to visit him and found him in a general ward. He was in good spirits, but he had lost half his body weight. He had cancer. The second time, he had been moved to a specialist ward. On the way I asked God for an opportunity to talk with him directly about the choice he was facing, but I could only do it if I was alone with him. As I arrived, I was dismayed to see a couple of others in the room, so while he small-talked I asked God to remove them. Two minutes later, inexplicably, the remaining man with a stroller and saline drip left the room. That was my moment to ask *N* if he wanted me to pray for him. This strong-hearted 59-year-old broke down in tears; "I'm so bloody scared, Si!" I asked God to give *N* the strength to get through this; an ambiguous prayer but I was walking on thin theological ice. My punchline was this: "Jesus isn't a nice guy in a nightie, *He's the Son of God*. The connection (to God) is with the Son!" He nodded and I left. The third time I went to visit, I realised what a window in time I had been given. *N* could now no longer speak. I asked him if he remembered our last conversation, to which he nodded slowly. The morphine must really have knocked him out. *R* asked me to countersign something legal and I departed. Before my next intended visit, I phoned the hospital ward just to check it was OK, and they gave me the news; "Sorry, he passed away last night." I cried of course, but I was also angry. Angry that for most of his life, he had not heard this thing called 'the good news', and despite moving in circles of physically tough men, it would take someone spindly like me to tell him how he could make the most important decision of his life, right at its very end. The decline was over within just ten days. I hope we meet again. Even if it's in the back of a Bedford MJ.

Declaration: Fear or faith

Fear. The great motivator to stay put or stop us dead in our tracks. It's worked its magic on me more than a few times, especially in the types known as 'fear of man' and 'fear of upsetting someone'. *People-pleasing* is a dreadful disease I have suffered from, and as its name suggests, it pleases everyone except me and keeps me enslaved to others' presumed opinions. I wasn't born to be a slave, and I wasn't born to live in fear. I was born to *live*. I write this understanding the current times we live in, where most people have fallen under the truck of fear.

FEAR. AKA 'False Evidence Appearing Real'. Whoever came up with that needs a clap on the back.

In the faith circles which I move in, there's a simple anthem which celebrates a simple truth: *"I'm no longer a slave to fear; I am a child of God...."* So, which is it to be? To be fearful or to be faithful. Fear keeps you as a prisoner. Faith sets you free.

Author's note: My prediction as of the end June 2021 is that mental health of many will plummet on the true understanding of the present times which will be revealed by the brave. In the months to come, certain facts will come to light which will shake men and women worldwide. When people realise what they have been subjected to, there will be shockwaves of disbelief and tears may flow onto the streets. My prayer is that it is not too late, and that repentance and healing will come.

Chapter Seven

A man in uniform

So many roles out there with so many distinguishing looks. Emergency services, military and airlines, through to the coastguard, prisons and railways. What is it that draws a man to a uniformed role? Is it the sense of identity? Is it standing for a cause? Is it pride in the uniform and job? How is that man affected by what he goes through, in the course of his service to the public and his country? Hereon I take a look at a few uniformed roles, because I too wore one, and I know what it is to be an ambassador for an organisation, to have to take the flack of occasional adversity yet with it, the moments of anxiety, depression and sometimes even despair. *Be warned, this chapter contains some disturbing and even gruesome details.

Paramedically speaking....

I was always told in my medical refresher training (called aviation medicine) that if ever you had a life/ death situation up in the air, you would always trust a paramedic even above a doctor. Why? Because their response training was constantly being updated. Sorry doc, it's nothing personal.

About 15 years ago, I fell into conversation with a man who was walking his dog along the canal side. John turned out to have been ex-Parachute Regiment and was a paramedic science lecturer. Of course he had some stories and told me the reason why I probably recognised him was that he was a featured persona on an air ambulance series. The one that has always stuck in my mind is this: a friend of his had attended an RTA (road traffic accident) where the victim was trapped between two vehicles. The fire brigade was there, as were the police and ambulance. The victim, a family man was effectively being held together by the cars as they pushed into him. John's colleague inspected all around and having conferred with all those present, he went over to the man who was being given medical attention. "You're being held in place by these cars. I have to tell you straight, I'm so sorry but there's going to be nothing we can do for you. When we pull the cars apart, you'll lose too much blood for us to save you. But it will be so quick you won't know it's happening." The man looked at John's friend and asked him to tell his wife and children that he loved them. In tears, the paramedic walked away, stood back, then gave the signal and the firemen started their machinery....

Shocking...(even) now

One of my acquaintances happens to be a former air cabin crew member. He's no Virgin to responder work. There are parallels between the air-based role and the medical response role. I can tell you straight, he's not just crew. Here's what he told me regarding a cardiac arrest and how he and others on the ambulance frontline have been affected. Over to Simon...

"My crew got called for this job where this 40-year-old had a cardiac arrest, a young guy. We didn't know it was going to be at a local football match, so when we arrived there were a lot of spectators, football supporters and families at this event...this guy had gone off and arrested. We spent about 25 minutes trying to bring him back to life and little did we know that his wife and his son were right next to us at that time. Very hard work and very difficult at that time. All we could hear in the background was his wife shouting; *"Save him, save him, please, please help, please help him!"* There were kids crying around us, you could see people's faces; friends, families, players all staring blankly, and as we were walking away it was quite surreal. We were doing everything we possibly could to get this guy back to life. It was a hard time for all the crews, we were very busy, all being used at that time. We had gone on longer than what we should have done. We usually go for 20 mins (with resuscitation) and if you don't get anyone back beyond that time we have to stop. We couldn't bring him back. Awful, awful...it was afterwards that what happened hit home more for me; it was his son being there and asking for his dad; *"Dad, Dad, Dad!"* It's just shit really. It will stay with me always... it will stay with me forever. It's awful. We got the patient to the back of the ambulance and the boy was at the side, still asking for his dad, and his mum and his friends were trying to push him away from the side of the ambulance. What struck me most is that I've got a family, I've got kids, it will never leave us... it's how important families are and loving people, it really is. I'm not a cold person, but that's the only time I've ever been truly upset after a job. Other jobs they've all survived, but this...it will always stay with us. It still affects me to this day, it makes me grateful to have my life and my family, I feel for his little boy and his wife.

Mental health? For people in the medical profession, it's a bit of a strange one and I can understand how it's going to affect different people I different ways. It affects me in ways it doesn't affect them, I can cope but it's always good to talk about it, I guess that's why I'm saying these things to you. It does make it easier the more you talk and share it, and if you bottle it up, it festers in your mind, so you have to share it with people, release it. Shit happens in your life and it's how you deal with it, bounce back and cope with it. And brandy does help as well, heh heh!"

I'm with Simon on that. (I'll also get help from *Courvoisier* and *Jamesons*.)

A Firefighter's reflection

Meanwhile, the rescuing continues. A firefighter I shall call *M* tells his story of a motorway pile-up and how he reacted as first responder. It's the image of the houseplant in the middle of carnage that gets me...

"With regards to significant incidents, I have always remembered the day of the week, never the month or even the year but always the day it fell on. Over my 25 years, I've attended many, some I've thought about and some I've forgotten by the next day. One incident in particular I've never been able to shake off, I remember so vividly and so much about it: the day of the week (Thursday), it was Easter 2002 and it was a bright warm day. The crew on that day had limited information and as we entered the motorway, it was already at a standstill. As we arrived, we had a plan, but the scene didn't fit. There were multiple vehicles, some in the 3 lanes with some off and it was filled with debris. I exited the rear of the appliance to see members of the public running about the carriageway when I was immediately grabbed by a female with shoulder length blonde hair. She grabbed me by my tunic over to a white Nissan Micra. The car was crumpled and had a single middle-aged lady with short red hair within it who was unconscious and clearly trapped. I vividly remember the blonde lady who dragged me there screaming at me that I had to help although she wouldn't let me go. I remember an overwhelming feeling that no matter what, I had to keep my head and do my job, even though I was on my own. After checking the lady was breathing, I explained to the blonde lady that I couldn't do anything unless she let me go which she then did. I was very much on my own and was desperate to find someone to help me but at the same time, aware everyone was concentrating on an HGV in the ditch to my right with multiple casualties. By chance at that point, as I started to remove the road rescue equipment, our probationer appeared to collect some kit. I quickly grabbed him and got him to assist me in carrying the then, very heavy combi tool to the crushed white car. We very quickly set up the tool and he then disappeared leaving me alone to work one again... The blonde lady remained and had now been joined by a Paramedic. Seeing this, I got to work and removed the driver's door which I was elated about as it came off quickly with minimal trouble. The sight within the car stopped me in my tracks as the injuries to the lady's lower body were nothing like I had seen before yet a house plant remained stood up in the rear seat completely unaffected by the massive impact. Worse than the sight of the horrific injuries was that the lady resembled by own Mum, particularly her legs. I battled to remove the lady who was semi-conscious and remember sliding her from her seat to my thighs as I crouched at the side of the vehicle. By now, a stretcher trolley had arrived, so I scooped her up and placed her gently down. I had a massive sense of achievement, a real feeling that I had made a different and all the training, experience and determination had linked together for that one job. It was at this point, as I still had these thoughts of elation, the situation changed. The lady started to fit violently, her very broken body starting to fail. I started to talk to her, giving her reassurance things were ok, but in my head I was saying *"No, no, no!"* Obviously, I wanted her to be ok, but I also didn't want that feeling that I had failed her. As the paramedic and blonde lady tried to rectify the situation, things got worse as the lady on the trolley stopped breathing and her heart stopped. As it was, the three of us helped as the paramedic did chest compressions. I did the bag and mask and the blonde lady helped by directing the moving trolley to an awaiting police helicopter which I hadn't even noticed land. The last time I saw the lady that resembled my Mum, was as she was loaded onto the helicopter. I had a glimmer of hope as I walked away when the Paramedic said she was breathing again. I went back to her car to make up the equipment, knowing I would probably be needed elsewhere as there were still other casualties. I worked on other vehicles with other individuals but have little recollection of them. I was solely thinking about the lady I'd helped and how she was doing.

A good hour later, when the dust had settled, I found myself back at the Micra sat on the crash barrier with a bottle of water. I contemplated whether I could have done things quicker and better than I had but was 100% confident I couldn't have, so I gave her the best chance. It was then the blonde lady returned to me. She explained she was a Doctor who was just behind the collision when it occurred. She told me I did a great job which made me feel good. She then placed her hand on my shoulder and said, "Her injuries were just too much, she didn't make it". This was my lowest point. I was happy with what I'd done, the medical attention she got and the timescale she got to hospital. In doing so, I had almost convinced myself, that all those factors meant she would survive, and the outcome would be positive.

Following the incident, I dreamt that night and due to the lady resembling my Mum, I felt I had to pay her a visit. This broke me, everything came out, every emotion. I had just burst out (crying) sat in my Mum's garden.

To this day, some 20 years on, I have not so much flashbacks but reminders. Obviously, seeing my Mum (her legs in particular) plus small white cars, takes me back. I still battle with if she had only dropped her keys, stopped for fuel or traffic lights, she would have been as little as five seconds ahead or behind, meaning she wouldn't have been in the wrong place at the wrong time. I feel on the day, I never got the support needed. This has driven me to be a diffuser, pushing the message that 'it's ok not to be ok', and offer support to others. It's taught me that you may at some point, suffer due to the job we choose, the people we are and the fact we get exposed to situations most don't. I'm glad the days of being a tough guy have gone because it's just not healthy. I'm not afraid to cry and I know if I did need help, I'd be the first to ask as the support is there. Just writing this, putting my thoughts into words has been a benefit. Sometimes, putting thoughts into words can act as therapy and it's helped me."

(*Author's note. NB. *M* still sees reminders. This is a very common thing with trauma and it's something I mention in 'A Saturday share'.)

This is your Captain speaking…

Soave, debonair, in-control. That's definitely not me. It describes a few of the captains I knew, but certainly not the one who Keith my favourite engineer described: "He looks a state, like he's spilt half his breakfast down his tie!" Captains and First Officers of the airline variety are just regular guys like you and I. Except when they get to fly widebodies, their wallets get bigger, they play more golf and they even dare I say it, get bored.

In my time in the airline industry, as a flight attendant, I started off in '96 with what could be called a cowboy outfit. The Lockheed Tristar we used was called

Alpha-Papa after the last two letters of the registration and in fairness was a pensioner, which is just how the car dealer described the VW Sharan he sold to me as he handed over the keys. *Alpha Papa's* job was to be in three different locations a day, according to the cowboys, but she was struggling to keep up with an impossible schedule. *'John Wayne'* and *'Lee Van Cleef'* happily took the dollars but cared little about the results. During that first six months of my time in the airline industry as a 'reluctant air steward', I experienced delays of an average seven hours per flight, anger, fights in the terminal, poor moods on flights which us crews managed to turn around and even journalists on board whipping up a storm among passengers for new tell-tale tabloid stories. *Alpha Papa* needed to go to the retirement home where she could look out the window and receive visitors once a week.

The captains who were allocated to our flights were ex-Royal Air Force, well-versed in military operations and warfare, and two in particular stood out as wonderful communicators. They would exit the flight deck to chat to punters on night flights, make public addresses to restore order in chaos, and even stand up on a table in Malta's airport to update customers who were now stranded there owing to technical problems (broken aeroplane). Captains have four rings on their sleeves to signify usually the amount of debt they are in times £25,000, the count of failed relationships they have had and the number of prestige cars they own or would like to own. (Don't take me fully seriously on these last points.) Senior first officers meanwhile have climbed sufficiently up the scale to show they are poised for future captaincy. They'll take the controls and sit in the left seat of the Jumbo/ A350/ 777/ 787 while Capitano goes on his/her break and that will give him/her the feel of being the main driver. For a couple of hours anyway. But what's going on inside their heads, these men of the skies who outwardly display good humour, airmanship and logic? Here's what *L* an American captain-friend of mine has come up with.

The personality profile of an airline pilot

L has been an airline captain for many years and is in his 36th year of commercial flying, mainly on Boeing airliners. This is how he describes the relationship between a pilot and stress-handling...

'Several studies have been conducted on the common personality profile of airline pilots as well as military pilots. For example, US Navy studies concluded that the personality trait of pilots are most identical to that of police officers and surgeons (anesthesiologist M.D.'s in particular). The personality trait commonality was based on how these professional groups handle stress during deeply critical moments. Of course, there are countless issues that can affect a pilot's mental health. However, one of the most stressful challenges a pilot can be faced with are those that involve behavior during life-or-death operational situations. A typical job description for an airline pilot can be summarised as a job consisting of *"hours of boredom occasionally interrupted by a few minutes of sheer terror"*. So how does an airline pilot successfully balance a (mostly) great routine job with moments that would give others a heart attack? Here are some personality traits a pilot must possess:

A "can do" attitude. An airline pilot must be completely confident, yet not cocky, in his or her own abilities. A typical pilot's attitude is that of "there isn't a problem I cannot fix". Staying calm and the ability to think clearly always are "must-have" traits of a pilot.

Pilots realise that training, and experience build further confidence, as one learns something new every day.

The ability to let go mistakes and successfully correct the mistake and move on when mistakes are made (yes, pilots make mistakes on the job like everyone else).

Taking control and remaining in control of any situation, applying the correct measures.

The ability and willingness to solve problems with his or her crew.

Not be afraid of using peer support and utilizing the airline's mental health support personnel if ever needed.

The ability to always leave personal problems out of the cockpit (or remove yourself from flying if the personal problems cannot be separated from the cockpit.)

Safety is always a pilot's number one priority.'

You can see the overriding themes coming through my friend's analysis of an airline pilot's state of mind. Problem-solver, critical thinker, methodical and capable. You shelve your problems before you check in...then once in the cruise, prepare to get bored."

Becoming a 'grounded' person

Christo is a former Q400 pilot who after a decade of flying commercially lost his job. With it, his outlook changed immediately impacting his own mental health for the worse. However, he was able to look at the positives and changed his course...

"When my passion was ripped away from me, it hurt. It really hurt! I could no longer escape the stresses and strains of life in my usual way. Instead, I numbed the pain with over-eating, drinking and unhealthy living. The short-term grieving process of redundancy took its toll on my mental health and reminded me of the pain and confusion when my uncle died by suicide when I was a young boy. I denied it was even happening. I was frustrated and angry. I bargained with guilt. This was followed by despair, grief and immense sadness. Then came the acceptance of the loss... and finally, the acceptance of hope. I have a loving wife, family and four young children that I need to care for, and whilst the process of recovery was not easy, I am aware of so many others in my position who have not had the support they need. I have come to view this period of 'uncertainty' as a time for gratitude, a fresh start, and new hope. Whilst the process of recovery was not easy, I am aware of so many others in my position who have not had the support they need.

Investigating the mind: Fortunately I soon realised that my role as a Black Box analyst and flight performance investigator had given me a unique skillset in tackling mental health issues... I was offered a role investigating events and trends from data received from the aircraft's "black boxes". I looked at why pilots were operating the aircraft outside of the usual parameters, and it was natural for me to always start the conversation with; "How are you?" The question usually prompted a flowing and personal narrative of what was actually going on behind the flight deck door. Just as the data analysis allowed me to unlock the black box's internals, a simple, open question gave me an insight into why pilots were behaving in a certain way. In establishing these relationships and taking the time to really listen, I found that there was always more to it with crew suffering from anxiety, financial worries, fatigue or relationship problems.

In aviation, these 'human factors', can build-up and lead to safety-critical failures. This is why pilots and cabin crew have strict checklists and procedures which keep everyone safe. Developing 'The Black Box Approach', I channelled my passion into developing a unique way of delivering accredited training programmes which deal with mental health issues in corporate and group environments. My presentation style is carefully structured, hugely empathetic and supported by his own personal experiences. In the training I passionately encourage open communication. This fuels connections and offers a lifeline to those in trouble. People do not always need answers, they just need to be listened to and be heard. Whilst many come on the courses to learn how to help others, they also learn how to help themselves. Learning the skills to approach uncomfortable subjects and listen to someone non-judgementally can help to create a happier and healthier society. By equipping people and organisations with the right tools and structures, I hope we can unlock the box and help end the stigma that surrounds mental health."

A pilot's journey

Steve is a pilot friend (heavy Boeings) whom I have known for nearly 25 years. I decided to keep his story just as is, with minimal interference. He has the perspective of several uniformed roles: the ambulance service, the airlines and although not mentioned here, the British Transport Police (BTP). Here's what he has to say...

"I am not used to writing this sort of stuff Simon, indeed, no experience with writing at all. So I will put my thoughts linked to my anecdotes and experiences down on paper. These are my recollections of incidents in uniform linked to issues of mental health and how it's dealt with.

Ambulance Service 1979-1984: As you know Simon, mental health was not a topic for discussion in general at that time. Many people obviously suffered in different ways. However, day to day, it was not considered (in my opinion)! An example that fits the bill for me is a harrowing experience I had one winters morning either November or December. It was snowing and the roads were like a skating rink. We received a 'shout' just on shift change over, 0700am. *"BABY, SUSPENDED BREATHING"* was the language control 999 used back then. We went as fast as possible, blue lights and 'two tones' but maybe only five to ten mph. Always in the back of your mind is *"what will I be faced with?"* Your mind naturally starts to play tricks and anticipation, apprehension and sheer worry all play a part until you are in receipt of the facts. We were confronted at the door with a mother and baby in arms SCREAMING and a father behind looking half dead with the most awful expression imaginable, not saying a word. We took the baby and off we went, I started CPR although the baby was stone cold and purple! Certified deceased on arrival by the consultant in attendance due to us placing a 'crash call' for arrival at A&E.

So why the big build up above, Simon? About an hour after that back at the station I went sick. We never did that back then, you just didn't. I was sick, cold, flu symptoms etc. Should not have gone in, but I did. Later that day I received lots of calls from crew mates having heard about the 'cot death'. They thought it was that, that made me go home. Looking back I think on the following :- was it psychosomatic? Maybe. Too long ago to tell, but the mind is a POWERFUL organ. Also, was this a form of 'crew' counselling me in our own way because no counselling was ever talked about, let alone offered.

We all used to share our 'bad job' experiences with each other then and they still do I am sure, and perhaps that was an 'in-house' was of dealing with stress, guilt (could I have done more), anger because you have no outlet. And laughter to break the mood and re-set you emotions through humour. A good friend of mine attended a 'railway job' in Watford, about a mile down the track from the station, Firemen, Police and Ambulance crew and train station manager etc.... All walking and not knowing what to expect following a train driver reporting that he thought he hit "something" on the track. They eventually found him on the bitterly cold night. So much blood that air smelt "metallic" and steam rising from what was left of him! Nothing was said for a long moment, then my mate David said, "Gentlemen, we can re-build him"! (A quote from a TV show at the time called *The 6 Million Dollar Man*!!) Everyone apparently erupted with laughter. False maybe. But it was a release from tension and sorrow, it 'lightened the mood'! It was further lightened with a roar of laughter when the Police searched him for ID only to find an INTACT bottle Guinness that had survived the impact.

We know that laughter is still used by cabin crew, pilots, in fact anybody that wears a uniform and has dealings with the public or things that may cause life changing situations. We do it now, as back then but have so many more coping mechanisms we can call upon if needed these days. The expression "laughter is the best medicine" still holds true, but back then that was pretty much all you had apart from chatting to crewmates and getting it off your chest so to speak!

I remember after the Kings Cross fire, so many firemen were traumatised, so they started counselling them. Maybe that was the start...I do not know. We were just left to get on with it. It's hard to know how something like that did, or still does affect you because it now forms part of your day-to-day life and existence. I want to separate the two, however after so many years it's impossible I think. I have so many other anecdotal stories about awful road traffic accidents back then, with people not wearing seatbelts... many, many fatal ones. One instance of a woman called Mary throwing herself under a train but not dying, and me spending time with them under a train until she could be stabilised and extracted. Many, many suicides, people committing suicide in different ways. But back then issues with mental health and counselling as I have previously said were not discussed, you just got on with it and, maybe because of that mindset, we did just get on with it and deal with it in our own way. Today there is far more mental awareness as you know and because of that, maybe the tolerance level is that much lower, and people are affected more, and to an extent seek out professional guidance and help on such matters. Rather like the 'Blitz Spirit' in the Second World War. *'Don't moan, don't complain, just get on with it'* was an attitude that we all look back on with some admiration. But not today because of the heightened awareness of mental illness and its possible fallout and not dealt-with or responded-to correctly. This was not my recollection back then. But back then in uniform and having to 'live up to' what that entailed and indeed was expected, leaves me with a sense of regret and resentment because I now have my 21st century hat on, it all seems so different because it is I suppose.

Airline Pilot 1991-present day: The thing about being in uniform back in the 80's compared to today (I believe) is that today having so much more awareness and the need, desire to bring it out in the open as opposed to 'sweeping it under carpet', makes for a far more healthy work / home environment. Obvious I know. BUT! This has made me think about aspects of why? Culture obviously played its part and an almost open 'macho' environment back then. The *'big boys don't cry'* attitude was strongly reinforced I believe back then, certainly if you were in some uniform or other.

You asked me about experiences on the flight deck with regard to how the situation was dealt with and what, if any, after affects were felt and handled. I think that without a doubt, the role of the Airline Pilot is so controlled, regulated, trained and tested these days (certainly in my brief time in the role) that the 'training does kick in' automatically to a very large extent, helps the outcome and how it affected you in the first place. Examples :-

Uganda is capital Entebbe. Just after take-off the right engine failed, and we had on board the vice president of Uganda. The training kicked in immediately and we started to fly the aircraft with one engine although we were very hot and heavy. The only option we had was to return to Entebbe, but we were very overweight, and the temperature was soaring. The classic hot, heavy and high.(Entebbe is 3,800ft above sea level). That information doesn't necessarily mean much to a person who doesn't fly but that combination is very hard to deal with. We also started to think that maybe the engine failure was sabotage, as this had happened in Africa before. This thought stayed with us all the way down. Events that later unfolded reinforced this thought, (see below) All three pilots were keeping a very close eye on the left engine. We came up with a plan to land at Entebbe. We would be landing about 30 tons over the maximum landing wait for that aircraft but could not dump all of the fuel that we wanted to, because that aircraft could only dump centre-tank fuel. The reason I'm going into some technical details of the events that day is to highlight the seriousness of the incident and the potential for an unfavourable outcome. Between the three of us we managed a successful outcome; due to the weight and temperature that day we used up nearly all of the runway to land. Just after we came to a halt all of the tires on the aircraft deflated. This was not unexpected however it is still a shock when it happens for real, as we have simulated this in the simulator many times. Then the left engine started complaining (low oil pressure)! This calls for the engine to be shut down, at this point we all became visibly disturbed. *'WHY has this happened? Did we miss something?'* Even, *'how will this affect us and our careers?'* So many thoughts, but the training was still at the forefront of our minds. We had a job to do, passengers and crew need to be attended to. This we did as per training (once again). Eventually, the passengers were taken to the terminal. It was at this point that it hit all three pilots, my legs became "wobbly" and I had to sit down. It came upon me on the aircraft steps, but I wanted to sit on the flight deck away from the crew! WHY? The macho pride maybe, not showing that we are still only human with natural human emotions openly. I don't know. But to my surprise, it had affected us all in similar ways. In an odd way, this helped us and allowed me/us to start dealing with the next "procedure" with an incident as difficult as this. Our own coming to terms with what and how it affects you in the aftermath.

The point of all this is the fact that even in the early 2000's, still no form of counselling was ever discussed or offered. We had a "tech" debrief with London later that day after all paperwork was completed and sent off to the authorities. But that's it. Maybe because it was not a "crash" but ultimately a satisfactory 'by the book' incident. I have lost count the number of times I have made single engine landings in the simulator, trying to fly 'by the book' and by the numbers to allow a PASS in that particular manoeuvre. But on that day in Entebbe as we passed 1000 feet to land, it suddenly hit me. WE ARE REALLY GOING TO DO THIS. Obvious I know, but that's the boundary between training (in the simulator) and the real world. But when it happens, it's a jolt. I still think back to that day now and again, not the worst thing to have happened to a pilot, but just about the worst for me!

A strange and VERY unusual incident that happened about 6 months after becoming a Captain on a Beech 200 Super King Air in 1992 affected me in a different way...Myself and a relatively new First Officer (who would later fly for a big airline, and would sadly commit suicide) were on our way to collect the New Zealand *Round the World Yacht Team* for the Vendee Globe Race (I think?) in La Rochelle. The plane had just had a big check, a sort of service and MOT. Three things happened, one after the other in quick succession that unnerved us to a great degree. 1. Passing 10,000ft the CABIN MASTER WARNING went off and the 'rubber jungle' (oxygen masks) fell. We donned our masks immediately (something I had never done before even in simulation) and requested a descent to a safe altitude. Once the checks had been completed, we discussed weather we could continue with the mission. We could but would have to re-file at 8,000 for the return and use more fuel. Not a problem! 2. However, about 2 minutes later, we had LOW OIL PRESSURE on the left engine. This required us to shut it down. Training again kicked in and this we did. We had to land ASAP, so elected to land in Southampton. But that was the end of the mission now obviously. 3. After completing our checks for a single engine landing, again something I had only simulated in the past, it dawned on me that this is for real. And I needed to 'step up' and get on with it despite the feeling that you wished that someone else would carry the responsibility. (The responsibility of command naturally.) However, when we put the landing gear down, we had an indication of 'two greens' not three! The right landing gear was not indicating down. So to cut a long story short, we checked with the Control Tower and Fire service equipped with binoculars and it "looked down". We landed keeping the gear off the ground as long as possible while keeping the aircraft straight and in balance, due to flying with one engine working, something I had never simulated before. We were both visibly shocked after the event and quite a while after. But once again, you just got on with it. Don't know what else to say really."

Cabin crew blues

Life in the clouds: it's a lot of tea and coffee certainly, turbulent sometimes, but I never let that get me down. Flight attendants in my experience have come from a rich array of backgrounds, and there is a noticeable interexchange of police and cabin crew. The attraction? It must be the uniform, shift work and public service similarities. Anything can happen, but most of the time it doesn't. Every time you hear a chime, your head instinctively looks upwards to see which of the four lights tell you the importance of the signal. You get used to working, eating and sleeping at odd times of the day and night. I found flying predictable in the main, but in the knowledge that something unplanned could happen at any moment. Could be a fire, decompression or a medical emergency for starters. A cheerful personality disguises hidden waters, as the job can impact your wellbeing mentally. You might never work with the same person again, let alone team. You could be away from home for days on end. You have limited choice over what routes you are rostered. If you have a problem with someone onboard and you can't rectify it, you're trapped in a tube with them until you land, and you still have to keep smiling in the interests of customer service and conflict resolution.

"Take care of yourself...don't suffer in silence"

D is a longstanding cabin crew member who runs his own website on the crew world. I asked him what his views were on the mental health of crew members and he gave some examples of how he has been affected by the behaviour of others. Don't suffer in silence is his ultimate advice.

"Some of the qualities one needs to be cabin crew include being approachable, friendly, warm, caring and a good team player. You're meant to plaster a smile across your face from the moment you put on your uniform to the moment you take it off again. But sometimes, behind the 'tits and teeth' there can be a whole number of issues simmering away under the surface.

When I was in my initial training, I remember one of the instructors telling us that we 'needed to leave all our problems at home, no matter how serious those issues were.' I remember feeling very uncomfortable with these words. Being told that I would need to bottle things up if ever I felt down or was potentially struggling with my mental health. But I was young, naive and desperate to be crew, so I sucked it up and nodded in agreement. Thankfully I quickly realised, after many late night and early morning conversations in the galley, perched on top of canisters or leaning against a bulkhead, that this wasn't the case at all. My colleagues would go on to become my friends, best friends, friends which your non-aviation friends simply don't understand the bond you have. Granted my initial training was over 15 years ago and things have massively changed since then with awareness around mental health being much more in the forefront of everyone's minds. Indeed, most airlines and companies today have numerous support networks or mental health programmes to assist employees should they require. Amazing I hear you say. Well yes, they are. I have used my own airlines peer support system and I have to say it really helped. However, to get that help I first had to go through my base/line manager. This person didn't have a clue how to support me, too busy attempting to force the reason for my recent absence out of me and tick a few boxes to report back to HQ. Despite my manager telling me they'd do everything they could to help me I left that office feeling worse than I had before. Thankfully, in the end I managed to bypass said-person and go on to eventually get the help I so desperately required. What was really frustrating was that I needed this help because of something that had happened in work involving a disruptive passenger. Sadly disruptive passenger events are an ever-increasing issue for crew around the world and one that is having a growing effect on crews' mental health, including my own.

I adore flying. I have done since I was a child. But after a particularly challenging few flights and little to no back up from my airline I was ready to hang up my wings for my own sanity. Thankfully, I managed to overcome my issues, for now at least. All I would say to any crew members struggling with mental health issues then please don't suffer in silence. There is lots of help out there. Just remember that your mental health is more important than that annoying passenger who shouted at you. That crew member who you don't get along with. That trip that you've been dreading and couldn't swap off or that captain that was horrible to you. Take care of yourself."

Flying vs family

The next story from a chap I know is typical of the struggle flight attendants have when there is a family crisis. You are in a role where you keep smiling, are focussed on the needs of others and stay upbeat. If you have a family problem, you don't inconvenience the business, but if you do, there can be a price to pay. Some feel penalised while they are trying to keep personal lives together. Double the stress immediately, compounding your issues. Over to N:

'I was due to sign in for my flight to Munich one afternoon, and while sitting in the crew lounge awaiting to check in, I received a text from my daughter. She was 15 or 16 and lived in Australia, and I in the Middle East (for work). We'd not been on the best of terms due to a variety of things, things that were really affecting me and not allowing me to focus properly. The text that she sent me was "I don't consider you as my Dad." I'm not sure anymore what triggered her to say this, but it stung me hard... I froze and felt something I'd never felt before – a mixture of emptiness, of dread and of helplessness. A feeling of failure and of being nothing. I had to call work the work hotline in this horrible state of mind, and say I couldn't go to work... I immediately felt and knew that I couldn't go on a plane to perform my duties as a flight attendant.

Because of the fact that I was calling so late, I had to be put through to my manager to explain my absence, who then told me I had to see a peer support officer immediately, and that my roster would say 'TBC' until such time that they had decided whether I should be classed as absent (a record you don't want in the company I worked for). My peer support visit was pointless; I was trying to get across my feelings to a voluntary peer support worker, who potentially had no experience of my situation. My emotions were up the wall, crying, angry, sad plus whatever else I was feeling, and all I got from the peer support worker gave me questions along the lines of 'what did you do wrong?' These very direct questions just compounded my stress and anxiety over a situation that I had no immediate control over.

From this, I really found it quite difficult to process the situation... I was away from my family, I couldn't just go to my daughter and talk with her about it, or at least just give her a hug about things... she was 11 hours away by plane, not somewhere I could just pop over to on a whim. In addition to this, I didn't have people around me that could truly understand my situation... most of my friends were younger, no children, so it wasn't something they could really relate to and offer proper advice. Of course their company was amazing, but I really found it difficult processing everything by myself, and not having my normal network around me to help me through it. I spent days and potentially weeks and months trying to process what happened – and still to this day I think about it... although today I have an amazing relationship with my daughter, and whatever happened that day is water under the bridge.'

Falsification at flight level 380: end of a career

K told me his story, which I had to edit down just for the sake of fitting it into this book, so some of it is paraphrased but the essence remains. He loved his role as is common with pretty much every flier. K's is not an unusual story to hear; years of dedication, high standards and loyalty rewarded by a kick in the teeth where your version of events is not believed. It could happen in any workplace sadly.

"Having spent most of my working life as cabin crew for (a major airline), I was made redundant in 2020 following the outbreak of Covid-19. I was on long term sick at the time but knew as soon as redundancies were announced that my cards were marked. During my 30 years with the company I never had a black mark against my name, always worked hard and was passionate about delivering exceptional standards of customer service. In later years as an on-board manager I worked closely with my crew to gain trust and respect, ensured procedures were followed and always tried to create a happy working environment. One aspect of my role that I particularly enjoyed was coaching and developing and during my twenty-five years as an on-board manager I wrote and delivered hundreds of performance reviews.

In 2003 a couple of years after being promoted to Flight Manager/ SCCM (Senior Cabin Crew) my partner at the time became gravely ill and I was suddenly faced with some difficult decisions. It was no longer possible for me to fly full time and part time was only available to female crew returning from maternity leave. Having told my manager I was considering leaving, he fought hard and managed to get me part time. Despite the turmoil of the next five years I remained loyal and committed to the company and put my heart and soul into every flight that I worked. In performance reviews written on me by colleagues throughout my time as an on-board manager I was described as professional, approachable and hard working. I took a keen interest in my development and spoke regularly to my manager about my performance. We had a great relationship, were open and honest with each other and he repeatedly told me I was a high performing member of his team. I'm someone who wears my heart on my sleeve and have always been thoughtful, kind and considerate. In my role as an on-board manager I understand the importance of rewarding outstanding performance but feel it's equally important to highlight areas where there's room for improvement. This is something the company has always encouraged. Sadly as I'll demonstrate, there are many crewmembers at this airline who don't take kindly to receiving developmental or constructive feedback. My manager and I spoke about this often because he also recognised it was a problem.

On 24th December 2018 I operated a flight to ATL Atlanta, a flight that I swapped onto and was one that changed my life. What took place over the next eighteen months was shocking and extremely difficult to comprehend. Almost three years later and I'm still struggling to come to terms with what happened. On that day unknown to me at the time, I checked in with five of the most vile and despicable people I have ever had the misfortune to encounter. My alleged conduct during the flight and whilst in Atlanta led to a complaint for bullying, harassment and inappropriate touching from a crew member still in his probation. Prior to joining the airline, he had been a serving police officer for eight years. He was on the flight with his now ex-fiancé, although I was unaware they were in a relationship.

Considering the seriousness of his allegations he said nothing to any member of the crew during either sector of the flight and nothing was raised with his manager upon returning home. I had found him to be aloof and unfriendly from the second we met which is extremely unusual in this company. I put it down to shyness, but it was some time before I discovered the real reason for his behaviour. I had allocated him a working position in First Class and during our pre-flight briefing he told me he had worked in that cabin many times. What I witnessed on both sectors of the flight showed otherwise and it was necessary for me to speak with him on several occasions about his performance. With him still being in his probation I felt it was important to write a performance assessment on him. Having received it he responded with accusations of bullying and harassment and accused me of inappropriate touching not only towards him but also towards other members of the crew. He made twenty-two separate complaints about my

performance, ability as a manager and overall conduct. Despite
proving unequivocally that this ex police officer, his fiancé and four other crew
members with whom they colluded were blatantly lying, the company upheld his
complaint against me. In fact very little of what I said in my defence was believed.
As a result of the huge amount of evidence that I submitted they struggled to
uphold any of the allegations but managed to uphold four.

Crew member *B* was a devious and malicious individual whose years as a police
officer enabled him to compile a deceptive and convincing complaint.
Furthermore he understood the importance of gaining support from other
members of the crew. *B* used facts from situations that had taken place and twisted
them which made the allegations extremely difficult to defend. Three other crew
members also accused me of inappropriate touching. One witness statement in
particular along with the one written by another crew member, was so personal
and venomous they have to be seen to be believed. All five witness statements
submitted by those trying to defend *B* were full of lies, inaccuracies and childish
nonsense. It was glaringly obvious that collusion had taken place. The remaining
three statements written by the crew who worked alongside *B* and I in First Class
told a very different story. There were three other crew members working in First
Class (excluding the crew member working in the galley). One was the longest
serving member of crew who had been with the company for eight years, the other
two had been with us for just over a year but had flown previously. These two best
friends had been at another airline for thirty years, twenty of which were spent as
on-board flight managers. Very little notice was taken of what these three crew
members said in their witness statements because it wasn't what the company
wanted to hear.

Irrespective of how much proof I provided the company refused to believe my
version of events and chose instead to believe two people who were engaged to be
married plus four of their friends. Four out of six in this group of hateful

individuals had been in the company for less than twelve months, another was on his second flight back after having been on a ground placement for a year. B's complaint was submitted three weeks after the flight, yet it was almost four months before witness statements were requested from the rest of the crew. They each received a questionnaire in which they were asked to respond to approximately 30 questions regarding my performance and conduct based on what had been claimed by B. Out of eleven questionnaires (including one to the captain and first officer) nine were returned.

As part of my attempt to clear my name I asked a doctor (of clinical psychology) whom I had been seeing for some time, to write to the grievance hearing manager regarding the accusations of inappropriate touching. His letter confirmed the allegations were unlikely to be true. His statement was based on matters that we had spoken about during consultations over the previous fourteen months. His letter made no difference at all and the response from both the hearing manager and senior manager who subsequently dealt with the appeal showed they were determined for this allegation to be upheld. In fact the response from the senior manager was quite unbelievable. In March 2018 I had returned to work after having been off for almost two years with mental health issues because of matters I was dealing with at home. Just nine months later and I was dealing with fabricated allegations of bullying, harassment and inappropriate touching from someone still in their probation who was aggrieved at having received a constructive report. That wasn't the only reason however why B felt such animosity towards me. The real reason was there in black and white in his own complaint and like so much else in this case, it has to be seen to be believed. In the months that followed I put together more than 600 pages of hard indisputable evidence, but the company had no interest in believing my version of events.

In May 2020 when redundancies were announced in response to Covid-19 I was told my job was at risk. I was on long term sick once again and had been since

December 2019. I was made redundant a couple of months later and subsequently received my P45 in the post. In true (*airline*) style it was the only piece of paper in the envelope and there was nothing else attached to it. It had been several months since I had spoken with my manager and the last email I had received which was from someone I didn't know, was to invite me to appeal the decision to make me redundant. I declined the offer. That was how my thirty-year career at (*the airline*) came to an end."

Facing the fear to look my ancestors in the eye

A current flight manager for a youthful airline which flies in red and white, Trevor told me his story. It's not what you would call predictable.

"Growing up as a young child, my brother and I were always put in the care of our grandmother in the school holidays at her large Edwardian house in the Hertfordshire suburbs, which pretty much looked the same in the 1970s, as it would have looked in 1900, My grandma wasn't one for wasting money or replacing things that weren't broken, so we still watched the TV she had bought at great expense in 1959. One of the things I always remember about the house were the many sets of black & white eyes that looked and followed me wherever I was in the room. Now you would think that would scare a young boy walking around an old house, but it didn't. You see, the images that followed me around were an excellent collection of family history on my maternal side, and became a great source of comfort and stability during an unsettled family life at home with both mum & dad partying as they would have done as teenagers in the sixties, rather than parents of young children in the seventies. This story is by no means an attack on them, they did the best they could do, after all their childhood had been wrecked by falling bombs on London, being evacuated, not even seeing their parents, and served rationing up until the late 1950s, so now that I'm older I totally get why they wanted to party. My grandmother kept a well-documented family history, going back to at least circa 1815, Some of the pictures were very large, and hanging on the wall over the fireplace, some were in frames next to the 1959 TV. One of my favourites was of my great grandfather sitting on a horse in his splendid army uniform during WWI, the other was of my grandfather who twenty later served as a captain of mine sweepers during WWII. You may well ask why these two images were in particular so important to me, and why two family members I would never meet could have a major impression on my life. One could go down a million routes as to why, but if I am being true to myself I could only call it shame and guilt that I had never had to give up my youth as they had done. Their peering eyes looking at me, as if to say, *"Do your duty"*. For the younger part of my teenage years I tried to do just that, in fact taking the lead from the young men in WWI, I lied about my age, and joined the Sea Cadets at ten, not the required twelve years old. For a time this served me well, I had a great time, and learned a lot about life, way more than my contemporaries walking the streets trying to look hard with their skinheads. You see along the Sea Cadets, we had the GNTC, which stood for the Girls Nautical Training Corps. Being a teenager, the main word that stood out there was of course Girls, and after having such a great time I was of course destined to join the armed forces, apart from it never happened, I don't know why. I think as I grew older, hanging with my mates on a Friday night drinking Woodpecker cider was more fun than military band practice, plus I had a part time job that took up my Saturdays and a couple of evening during the week.

Even when I went to University this sense of guilt was still hanging over me. The same pictures still looked at me every time I visited my grandmothers houses, she was looking older, while the men in the pictures didn't look any older, It was as if I was living a real scene in Dorian Gray. I tried to correct this guilt by enrolling in to the Officer Cadet Training corps at University only to be kicked out a couple of weeks later for punching a fellow recruit after he had the audacity to criticise a bridge I had built during an exercise starting at 2am on a very cold rainy night on Holcombe moor. If only he hadn't been so rude, my life could have been completely different...With the British Armed forces growing smaller, and my age becoming bigger, I decided I had left it too late to join the military, and by an accident of fate, I was going out with a fellow graduate who had become an 'air hostess' for a year or so before she settled on a 'proper career.' I found I was suddenly attracted by this career, after all, you got to see the world, stayed in beautiful hotels, met the most wonderful people.... Oh and you were paid. I decided to join myself. The girlfriend at the time went mad, it was ok for her to do it, but not me. I joined anyway, although it took me a couple of attempts. For the first few years it was a party, the airline I worked for knew how to party, we were in fact encouraged to party, and we did! I soon became a tad bored with the parties and settled down with the most wonderful girl, and we have three gorgeous daughters, unlike my parents I didn't party around them, no need, it was already out of my system.

Then a series of events happened that affected the airlines, SARS, Bird flu, 9/11 Ebola. What the airlines were finding is that no crew wanted to fly to these places, but I was totally the opposite, I couldn't wait to volunteer, my friends and family said I was totally bonkers for wanting to go anywhere nears these destinations. For example 9/11, I was watching live when the second plane went into the tower, all flights were stopped, but when they did start going back, many crew did not want to fly there, even though with the extra security it was most likely the safest time to fly. I did volunteer, and I was on my airline first flight back. It was a very quiet flight, not only in numbers, but the volume of noise. It turned out that most of our passengers were either relatives of those who had been killed, or British firefighters and police who had also volunteered to help. Even though I knew there wasn't physically much I could do to help, I really wanted to do more than just fly people out there, but I knew my only part was to get the family's and services to NYC. I will never forget how different the atmosphere was in the city that never sleeps. I had a few private moments to myself, as the live images were still fresh in my head of the second plane going into the tower, and people jumping off rather than being burnt alive. Haunting. Flying never went back to 'normal' after that. The same thing happened with the Ebola crisis: the airline was finding it very hard to crew these flights. Again I volunteered, I found the whole thing really exciting, not that I ever mentioned that at the time. I'm not sure why I did, I guess I was feeling I was at the centre of world events, but I should also mention these flights were really easy, as everyone was so compliant They just sat in their seats, they didn't drink, they didn't moan as they normally about the small stuff.

Now we arrive at the now..... 2020/21. I had seen the build up to the Covid crisis way before it was even mentioned on the mainstream media, as bit by bit real news filtered out of China, and not that was put out by the propaganda arm of the Chinese Communist Party(CCP). Real news soon seem to stop, as the social media companies soon complied with the orders of the CCP. When Covid did arrive in the UK, I was already convinced that I had had it, as I had been feeling really ill, although I thought it was malaria due to the amount of times I spent on the West Coast of Africa, and malaria was a big thing we were being taught in aviation medicine during our yearly safety exams. I was so convinced that it was Malaria, that I purchased a malaria self testing kits from Amazon which required a pin prick of blood, but it always came back negative. Even though I knew of Covid, it slipped my mind that I had been in Shanghai on a long trip in December 2019. I think I was too busy buying Christmas presents for my girls rather than thinking of Covid.

In March 2020 It happened. I landed back from West Africa knowing the country would be entering lockdown for two to three weeks to 'flatten the curve'. For me I was glad. I was knackered, and I really needed the rest, I also felt this was a great moment of destiny, and no matter what happened, my life would never be the same again. Even then I wondered if I had watched the film 'Young Churchill' once too often, as he was always into destiny, also as I had written before I was convinced I had malaria so I could have been a bit delirious, but either way this imposed rest was welcome, after all it was the hottest March/April for a long time.

The garden looked wonderful, so there wasn't much not to like. Those weeks turned to months. I was ready to do something, those jobs around the house had been completed, then one morning on the news a story appeared that grounded aircrew could be used to work in the newly constructed Nightingale hospitals, as soon as I heard this I email my manager to see how to apply, he didn't know, but I did, I can't remember how. I waited, I filled out their long forms, and nothing happened, we were never used. I did however sign up to another scheme using aircrew called *Project Wingman*. Now these guys were impressive. I believe they went from drawing board to have over fifty lounges within weeks. My family were a bit worried about me bring Covid into the house, but I had to do it. I was given a fantastic placement with other crew from many different airlines, nearly all I remain in contact with. The sad part of all this was seeing the aviation world collapsed, and crew who had been working for the same airline for over thirty years suddenly had lost their careers, crew who had resigned themselves that they would be crew until retirement, now had completely new careers, many within the NHS.

I have so far been one of the lucky ones, and at the time of writing I am still employed, all be it on furlough. I haven't been lazy, and I have been very busy working on other projects some of which have changed my world. Even though I was placed on furlough, the airline was still very keen on us to remain in check on our aircrafts, that way if the skies did suddenly reopen they would have a bank of crew ready to fly. As part of this we had to fly one supernumerary flight to remain in check. I was given a three night Tel Aviv. Wow... the beaches and hotel were beautiful there: a quick flight and it would be so nice to receive some allowances again. What can I say, the flight was lovely, not very busy, a fantastic crew. We had heard on the news that trouble was brewing between the Israelis and the Palestinians, and we joked we would have to dodge the missiles as we landed. As it happened it was a perfect landing, we arrived at the hotel at 6am. The younger crew were ready to hit the sun, I was ready for bed.

After four glorious hours of sleep I hurried down to the pool. It was so nice to be back. The younger crew were already on the sauce. I held out, until a crew member shoved a neat shot measure of gin at me. After that, what was going to be a relaxing few-hours by the pool, became a beach party just down the road. I thought I hadn't missed flying, but this brought a real smile to my face, although after a few drinks, I realised I couldn't party the way I used to, and was more interested in getting back to the hotel for the buffet. So along with the flight deck and another older crew member, we headed back to enjoy this delightful feast served with a lovely selection of red wine, which they kept on bringing us. Not long before I was ready for bed, I saw many people being ushered out, and at first thought it was later than it was, and the restaurant was ready to close, apart from it wasn't. As one of the staff opened the thick double glazing doors, I thought I had been transported back to the blitz, as all I could hear were air raid sirens. We were ushered, not forcibly, but in a method that gave us no choice but to go downstairs into a bunker that I had no idea existed. I don't know why, but my first reaction was to grab the newly placed bottles of red wine and two glasses. A feeling of excitement came over me, and I was ready for when the bombs hit, as my mind ran over first aid training. I was also concerned about my fellow crew members who were still out partying, but with modern communication, it wasn't long before we found out they were safely in a bunker in the other hotel block across the road. Knowing they were safe, I really wanted to see more. while in the bunker, we were chatting with the security guard. He could see I found the whole thing exciting (a strange feeling, as I knew other people were on the other end of these dropping bombs) He had to go to the roof of the hotel as part of his checks, I asked him if I could go with him. I never thought in a million years he would let me, but he did! Going out on that hotel roof was the most surreal sight I had ever seen. How can something so destructive look so beautiful? The Israelis call it *Iron Dome*. A defence system which intercepts incoming rockets. I don't know if you've ever seen the film *'Apocalypse Now'* in which the character Major Kilgore is on a beach during a battle with bombs going off around him, and in the words of the commentator, "He knows he would not get so much as a scratch"? That's how I felt for that brief time I was up there. Most likely due to the extra red wine I had consumed. The bombs stopped that night, and the next day, after a great sleep (how), the world around us acted as if nothing had happened, even the Israeli version of 'Just Eats' was still delivering. Then as soon as night-time came, so did the bombs. The poor airline must have been pulling their hair out as to how to get us out of there. We had another two nights of this, with only one daylight bombing raid. I still had this feeling of excitement and adventure.

Eventually the company came up with an evacuation plan to fly us to Cyprus on a El AL commercial flight with other customers, The crew were lovely to us, we were in full uniform. Even though it was exciting, I suddenly felt relaxed when I saw that we were leaving the Israeli shoreline. In Cyprus we were put into a lovely hotel for three nights. Someone told me it was for decompression purposes (the company wanted us to have some R&R to get over what had just happened, before we went back to our families) Someone else said it was because there were no flight...... I would like to believe the former. The BA crew that brought us back to the UK were fantastic, absolute uniformed comradeship from one airline to another. Arriving home was lovely, a real hero's welcome, apart from I hadn't done anything, but hoping I would have if it had gone horribly wrong. I'm sure I would have, which I why I can now look at my uniformed ancestors in the eye, well almost!"

Line of duty (*warning: it's graphic*)

P was a cop since the age of 21, fresh-faced and eager, who went onto become a DS in anti-corruption and witness protection. He's no bent copper, feller. Here's his tale of the impact of what he saw, which you'll see still affects him.

"I thought the best thing to do is tell you a couple of my 'war stories' from my time on the force and let you take it from there and do with it as you see fit. I guess it's fair to say that these two events had a lasting impact on me as they occurred when

I was a young uniformed PC in the late 80's/early 90's and yet these are two of the tales I would always tell when sat on a canister in the rear galley on a deep night flight and my colleagues would ask me about my former job.

The first tale that I am going to tell you about occurred on a summer's day midweek '2 – 10' shift and I was out on mobile patrol on my own, which was usual as we only paired up on night shifts at that time. It had been a quiet shift and around 9pm I decided to head over to our HQ where we had two petrol pumps (long since gone) to fill the panda up ready for the night lads. I recall that as I pulled into the entrance way a car came speeding in behind me flashing it lights and beeping its horn. I naturally stopped and the guy jumped out and said I needed to come quick there had been an accident just up the bypass from where we were. I remember saying that I'd just quickly fill up and then go and see but he said, 'No, you've got to come now, it's bad!' Naturally I took him at his word and jumped back in the car and headed out onto the A59 bypass and turned left towards Southport. The road was a dual carriage way at that point and less than half a mile up the road, it went over a hill where it crosses a minor road below. As I crested the hill, I'll never forget the scene that I saw before me. The best way I can describe it was like something from a disaster movie set with cars abandoned in all directions and numerous bodies lying in the road, on the verges and hanging out of cars. I naturally radioed in to ask for urgent assistance and the ambulance service and then before I knew I was at the scene and those that were still conscious immediately looked to me, a 'wet behind the ears still' 24-year-old to take control and make everything alright! I later was told that a car full of young people had been speeding and the driver lost control and crossed the central verge where it collided head on with another car full of people going the opposite direction. There had been a number of other collisions as other cars swerved to try and avoid the mayhem that was unfolding in front of them.

I don't think I'd ever even dealt with an injury RTA before let alone anything on this scale. (They used to be called RTA's - Road Traffic Accidents but are now RTC's - Road Traffic Collisions, on the premise that any such collision occurs as a result of someone's actions and are not accidental).

No training could have prepared me for this, not that I had been given any other than basic first aid during my initial 16-week spell in the training college and how to fill in the correct accident forms! Common sense kicked in and told me that the ones who were making the most noise were possibly the ones in least need of my immediate help and that it was the quiet ones I needed to check on first. The first couple of casualties I checked were clearly dead and then I found a guy who was still alive and knelt down and cradled his head as he took his last breaths, before lying to his girlfriend and telling her he would be okay and to just hold him to make him comfortable. I managed to get another guy into the recovery position and another one who I later found out survived as I did my best to make him comfortable in the middle of the road. I had no equipment, little training and was on my own and could only move from body to body, doing the best I could for them. It was probably only 10 minutes until the first car arrived to help me and not much longer 'til the first of many ambulances arrived, but it seemed like an eternity. As soon as the cavalry had arrived, I was told to go and write up my pocket notebook about what I had found and what I did. I went back to the nick and did this before finishing my shift, went home at 10pm as planned, and turned back into work at 2pm the next day with barely a word said about what I had done, what I had seen and what I was feeling. I guess counselling just wasn't a 'thing' back then.

At the time I suppose I didn't realise what impact the events of that day had on me, but I guess that as I am wiping away the tears as I write this over 30 years later, it's safe to say it had a significant and lasting impact.

The second 'story' I can tell you about occurred around two to three years later after I moved again to another local town midway in size between my first and second posting. My sergeant here was a tough guy, a proper 'man's man' who I recall liked to race rally cars in his spare time. He was a veteran of around 20 years' service, and we were mainly a very young shift of around five or six PC's maximum, usually less due to leave/sickness etc. We were working nights when a call came in in the small hours that a train driver had reported colliding with something, probably a person, on the railway line on the way into Preston Train station. It was agreed that we would climb down onto the tracks from one railway bridge and British Transport Police (BTP) would climb down from another bridge further up and we would search the tracks and meet in the middle. The shift all came together on a quiet country lane and with Dragon Lamps in hand we clambered down on to the tracks. We stayed together as we walked towards the next bridge to meet our BTP counterparts and as we went it quickly became apparent that it was a body, or body parts that we were looking for as we were finding bits of intestines and internal organs as we moved along the tracks, as well as a foot still in the shoe. I remember being amazed at how pink and glistening the intestines were between the tracks as we shone our torches on them. It wasn't long before we came across the main part of the torso, which was mainly naked, as apparently being hit by a speeding train tends to rip your clothes off. This was just the trunk of the body with no legs and no head and it was our Sergeant who came out with the line that 'when we find the head, he will definitely have dandruff as he has lost his *Head and Shoulders'* (famous shampoo). We all found this hilarious and despite the grim task we were in good spirits as we went along collecting the various body parts into the bin liners we had brought along. After a few hundred yards the unmistakable back of a human head was spotted at the trackside and being the leader, our Sergeant went over and picked it up by the hair and held it aloft like a scene from a zombie movie. He held it up proudly face towards us and then turned the head towards himself before dropping it and falling to his knees and wailing. It turned out that he was holding the head of a close family member! We quickly got him back to the station and another Sergeant from a neighbouring town came over and took him home while we asked BTP to finish the task of collecting the remaining body parts.

It's fair to say that *G* the Sergeant, never fully recovered from that night and although he tried to come back to work after a short spell off, he could no longer hack it and I believe he was medically retired a few years later due to the emotional impact it had upon him. That night didn't particularly impact upon me as it wasn't my relatives head that was being held aloft and the fact that we had all been joking about the body previously wasn't unusual as it was perfectly normal for police officers to deal with the stress and trauma by making jokes and using dark humour. A typical example would be going along to deliver a death message to a loved one, on the way you would joke that you were going to knock on the door and say, 'Are you the widow Brown. No? Well you are now.' I heard this line numerous times during my service but of course when you get to the house, you instantly got professional and serious and dealt with the matter sensitively. The only thing I never heard any officer joke about was a death or serious incident involving a child or baby, these were definitely off limits for joking around.

It's probably been a little bit cathartic for me to sit here and write it down and realise just how much that first incident impacted on me and how little (none) support I received at the time."

P's tale must be so typical of what police officers have to deal with, and the fact that he's so emotional all these years later is very revealing.

You're in the army now...

So, what of our friends in the military? It's pretty well-known that many ex-soldiers have struggled to adapt to civvy-street, and some even end up on the streets. What a reward, for serving your country, and that's without loss of limbs or

PTSD in the picture. Imagine that you have been drafted to a foreign country in the intense heat of a warzone, to fulfil a peace-keeping role or fight an insurgency. You spend maybe a year or two away from home, in the company of others in the same boat, sometimes fearing for your existence and witness horrifying events. You wonder about your kids and meeting your new-born son for the first time ever. You wonder if she's missing you or if she's found another while you're gone. Your duty is extended. You feel powerlessness. You come back to your home country, normality and people moaning about little things. You don't sleep and can't process. The adjustment must be colossal.

Baked in Baghdad

I can tell you from my own experience as a civilian, imagining how this played out for US soldiers of the 101.st Airborne Division based in Baghdad, Iraq July 2003. For several days, I knocked around with a few, as three of my friends and I were taken under the wing of one of the Majors, patrolling streets of the capital in a truck, sitting in on military briefings and visiting their heavily-securitised compound. (Four of us had landed there by UN plane from Amman, Jordan and experienced the baking-oven heat as soon as the doors were opened. *Sadaam International* was a hive of intensive military activity, ranks of impressive-looking helicopters and bulbous transport aircraft cooking in the sun that beat mercilessly down on everything. We were escorted by soldiers across the apron to the hangars which had been converted into an arrivals/ security hall, where our names were taken, we were body-searched, and our bags checked for weapons.)

The general mood was one of relaxed alertness in the heat of the Middle East's most dangerous cities. When I talked with tank-crews, whose vehicles were usually covered with netting under palm trees, they told me they had ways of keeping themselves cool while in full body armour, under the baking of a relentless oven that was Baghdad. When I talked with soldiers as they removed their helmets awhile, they missed their families, friends, their hometowns, cold beers and BBQs.

However, you could clearly see they were ready for a quick change in the atmosphere. Bill said to me that while we were being driven, he watched the Major sitting in his front seat observing all around as we drove, *but his hand was never off his pistol.* They were resigned to the fact they had a job to do, as I watched them in their daily duties pulling cars over to perform weapons-searches, to distributing water bottles to locals out the back of their *Hummers,* while *Black Hawks* and *Chinooks* flew over the city, reminding us this was a live warzone. They took us to meetings of Iran-Iraq war-veterans, local hospitals and even to one of Sadaam's old palaces which had been looted but was still obviously a place of splendour. I passed overturned and burnt out cars, destroyed tanks, convoys of UN marked 4x4s and lorries, bombed telecommunications buildings and regular life going on with packed food markets and queues over a mile long for a gas station. Can you imagine making the transition from there to the everyday world we live in? Can you understand how the soothing voice of a wife, girlfriend or a partner from many thousands of miles away would give comfort to you in this hell-hole? It was the heat and the dust I'll never forget, and these guys lived in it for months and months. They were tough alright, and they had to be. Mentally, not just physically. I told one of them he reminded me of Huey Morgan from *The Fun Lovin' Criminals,* but he had never heard of them. (Huey was a former US marine, so the comparison was clear.) Loco.

Rockets to normality?

P was working in the Air Force during 2008 in Iraq and his story centres around seeing a close colleague become a victim of Indirect Fire (IDF) Rocket Attacks. He speaks of how he failed to deal with it, and how his anger spilled out until someone came alongside him to help him through the pain...

"Deployed in Iraq on a 4-month deployment with the Royal Air Force, my second deployment to the same base in just over a year. The tempo was very different, unlike the first deployment when we had our weapons in the armoury, minimal body armour within the workplace and sleeping in tents. This time we carried our weapons when every we left the office, wore our enhanced body armour when out of the buildings, it now had to be beside us and able to be put on quick time, our sleeping accommodation had certainly changed, this time it was similar to Porta Cabins with sandbag on the roof, defences around the outside and the bedding area it's self was breeze block with a small aperture to climb in, the top was made of steel and covered with sandbags, again our weapons and body armour to hand. What was the difference? In my last deployment there were approximately 50-60 IDF attacks, usually no more than a couple of rockets at a time, however this time they were being fired at us in Salvo's up to 15-20 at a time. In the end in my last deployment, I ended up with a count of IDF just short of 500. The incident which sticks in my mind, which changed me as a person, although I did not see the changes, happened late in the evening.

IDF incoming and the unit being defended by an awesome bit of kit which engages the rockets within a set range and destroys them. On this particular evening the defences worked, destroyed the incoming IDF, however the destroyed rocket fell extremely close and hit the person near me, unfortunately this resulted in his death. I knew this person and was unable to inform any others of his fate. In the morning the unit commander gathered the fallen brother's section together to inform them of the evening tragic event. He was a very well-respected person and only had a short while left in Iraq, he was my section leader. There was total shock and to make it hit home even harder, there was another IDF attack shortly after the commander had informed us. Lots of the junior members of the section were shaken up that's for sure. The lip service of help from the Padre (person of the clergy) was mentioned.

Upon return back the so-called normality I was told that if I wanted any time off, I could ask. This is when family started telling me I was not myself. I was short tempered and on occasions could be downright nasty. I of course did not agree. I discovered a taste for a certain red grape liquid product. Looking back, I guess it was the feeling of guilt, why him? How was I so lucky and he wasn't?

It was sometime later when attending a function that the Padre of my home unit found me holding up the bar. He asked how I was doing, of course I replied I was fine, but being the great person and judge of character he was, he leant forward mentioned the name of my fallen brother and said I was talking rubbish, and I guess he was correct as I felt the tears run down my face and we both left the room. The Padre was a great person and took several hours out of his very busy day for the next few months to discuss and talk things through with me. I sorted myself out and joined the HM Coastguard on-call 24 hours to give me a focus and this prevented me from having a drink. I gave 10 years of service to the HM Coastguard before leaving due to family and work commitments. I did several courses to aid others if they every needed anyone to listen to their problems and help prevent them feeling the way I did.

How do I cope these days after leaving the RAF? I have joined the Ambulance service, helping others, my marriage came to an amicable end, I have a lovely soul mate who makes me extremely happy, a supporting family and I get out on my motorbike to clear my head and keep those awful memories in boxes tucked away at the back of my mind."

Closer than close

P worked in the military police and also trained in Close Protection duties, having guarded the then-PM and other diplomats. He's a genial man whose demeanour busts traditional military stereotypes. This what he recalls....

"I would say that when I served in the military, it was pretty bad when it came to Mental Health awareness. Despite what was learned from the first war to the second war in terms of shell shock. There was a macho environment that also included women too - no one could admit weakness. I remember one nightshift as a Military Policeman - a 14-hour shift. That night, I dealt with an aggravated assault, a burglary, RTA (as they were called then) and a suicide. My duty Sergeant's words of comfort were, "Make sure that Land Rover is clean and fueled, before handover." I went to bed, tried to sleep. That night I was back on again like nothing had happened whereas that poor woman now had no husband. We used to stick together, and it was my mates that helped me. We would get drunk and talk. Also, I was obsessed with fitness and this was a great release too. That was General Police Duties.

I trained in Close Protection and noticed that this side of the military was very different. Everyone was on first name terms. You could be in charge of an operation as a Corporal and people senior to you, in rank, would report to you. A lot of ego was removed plus, there felt like there was more genuine support there. Of course, with any specialist training unit, you would get egotistical people but, for the most part, you could only get away with that if you were superb at what you did. In my experience, the true heroes I met were very modest - they did not want to talk about how many people they had to shoot. I was lucky that I never had to shoot anyone although and I left the military pretty unscathed, so I was very lucky. I found it gave me great for me. Some of my colleagues still walk around with invisible scars and regrets in their heads - which torment them still."

Escape to victory

P relayed his tale to me of being a soldier in the army (European country) feeling like a secret agent. As a gay man, he was not welcomed any longer at his own family home and actually escaped from his parents. Imagine it being so bad at home, he felt forced to run... He joined the army as a full-on conscript, not just the usual national service for a year. He was at odds with the part he played in his military career of four years. He told me he felt like a spy, as a sergeant in the army where he kept his private life quiet. He now does something completely different professionally in the field of therapy. The feelings of the past don't go, and he remembers them constantly.

De-Construction, re-laying the foundations

Ok, not quite a traditional uniform, but I will argue that PPE counts as such. It's now no secret that in a realm dominated by *men's men*, it has become harder for males from bricklayers to foremen, to speak out and become tender. If you use a power-drill, a JCB or even a crane, then you are officially *a man*. A man who is self-contained, can laugh with the boys, take the p*** out of others' workmanship and clock-off from the site at 5pm for happy hour. But what if you're shielding your inner pain and your environment won't allow you to share your vulnerability? Yes, CDM covers health and safety, but barely touches *mental* health and safety. There is a crisis of poor mental health in the construction industry which has resulted in soaring numbers of workers feeling they have no option left but to dispatch themselves to leave the pain behind. You could be a civil and structural engineer, a clerk of works, a joiner, a plasterer or a brickie and be chronically affected because you feel the industry doesn't allow you to speak. With no one to open up to, the loneliness and the darkness can become too much.

Left cold in the Antarctic

Paul is a construction project manager with decades of experience, most recently in the Middle East. However, the story he relayed to me was of a colder climate, with two tragedies, where two men on his team just couldn't cope, ironically just at the point they were about to return home to the UK from the bleak white canvas that is Antarctica.

"So the job was a two-year contract to build an Antarctic research centre; totally remote. We had to take a boat all the way from Hull, right the way down the Atlantic to the Falkland Islands and then onto a place called Rothera. We had to take absolutely everything with us, there was no backup if we forgot something we had to make do. So the logistics and the preparation was massive, in fact the only thing that we forgot was the mustard! We took two entire boatloads of gear, plant and equipment and the first thing was to build our own camp on the ice. Everyone was living on the boat while we built a camp, and we did that in two weeks and then we started the construction. Concreting at minus 45 is rather difficult; heated water insulated, form work chemical additives, heated blankets over the top, all that sort of thing. It was a very bleak and we prepared everything from the construction part pretty well, but the one thing that we didn't allow for, and I as the project manager never planned for, and didn't have any training in, was that my main role was not as an engineer or even as project manager, but it was a welfare officer. The biggest problem was the total isolation with nothing to do except work. No internet connection, no phones; letters were possible if for some tourist ship happened to be in the area that had come from the Falkland Islands. For the 40 or 50 guys we had down there, during season one we were doing all groundworks putting in drains or whatever. Yes, it was impressive to sit there in a nice warm, cosy pub in the middle of Birmingham, saying you were going to work in the Antarctic, surrounded by thousands of seals and penguins, but the grim reality is when you're actually exposed to it and there's nothing else to do, and you can't talk to your family and friends; just the blokes you're working with and living with, and it doesn't get dark ever (it's daylight 24 hours a day), and there's a very tight programme with obviously no extension of time: if you haven't finished you can't get more time. You've just gotta get on the boat and go home, make sure we have finished, regardless of what the weather threw at us.

There was this one particular chippie, he was a young father, and desperately regretted coming down but there was no way of getting him back. He worked well, but he was a loner and spent most of the evenings on his own and I don't know what was going on in his head, but he was in charge of four other blokes...they were a bit behind. They could have hit the target... and it all got too much for him. I don't know what it did to his brain, but he actually finished the job, we got the boat back to Port Stanley and we had to wait there for a couple of days because the weather wasn't very good. We had to get the RAF flight back to Brize Norton, and then sadly he took his own life on the island. Just went out in a car...I think he gassed himself. No note, nothing, and that was pretty traumatic for the whole group.

The other guy, he was actually an engineer in charge of a site that was quite remote, a few days boat away. I was able to talk to him on CB radio in the evenings With about three weeks to go, he sounded like he was cracking up. The pressure was getting too much for him, and he had a much smaller crew; they had about 16 of them. In the end I thought I had better get a boat and go and help him to finish the job as we didn't think he was going to be able to finish. Two days before I got there we found that we found he had strung himself up in his office. The amazing thing was he had actually got the job completed. Without the support, and the pressure being too much, he decided he couldn't face going on. It was right at the end of the job, and within a few days he would have been united with his family. Pressure, isolation, no contact with loved ones... and it does strange things to a man's mind."

Developers have similar issues. Someone I know of builds high end properties and faces the invisible pressure on his thoughts daily. From what I know these are typical concerns: *My backers are asking questions. Will my project succeed? Materials are now costing double; even a bag of plaster that cost £4 a few months ago is now £8/ bag. The cost is being passed onto me. Will all my houses sell? Will I break even? Will I go under...? Can I pay my workers? Can I feed my family?* Another developer I know has fled the country completely to take on a business development role in the USA. More than likely he saw the market was going west so to say....

Build me an airport

R is an airfield technical and compliance manager/ construction manager for a regional airport. He has a history of mental health issues and wanted to highlight these experiences to other men to help them. There is he says, a stigma, but he wants to help even if it's just one person. His triggers were fatigue and stress following the birth of his first child. He had a social anxiety when taken out of usual familiar inter-professional comfort zones, for example when arranging to meet new contacts for something even so simple as a coffee and a chat. His family life was impacted badly. He would shake, sweat, exhibit headaches and nausea. Training courses would convince him everyone was looking at him which would increase his near-paranoia. His anxiety was baseless but real; he says he "was more anxious about being anxious." Coming to the point of realising he had to address it, this triggered him almost breaking down in front of his line manager. The result was he was given six months off the business, a career-break. R tells me that owing to the impact of COVID, remote 'virtual' meetings have actually had a huge positive result for him. Previously he used to suffer social anxiety from attending meetings and seminars that used to be away from home. He is now in a stronger position, able to confront his fears and meet them head-on. He's fully compliant and oversees excellence in runways, among other airport facilities. He's on a (take-off) roll.

Off the rails

When you think of train drivers, I'll bet the thought crosses your mind about how many suicides they must see in the course of their careers. Bridges, open land, platforms, level crossings, in fact anywhere a person could feasibly access tracks, could be used for this most devastating and final event. But what of the impact on the driver? M is a driver-mentor, and this is his story...

"I suppose the most traumatic incident I've had, and most drivers have is a suicide which is referred to in the trade as *'having had one under'*. It was around 4 years ago I suppose, a lovely sunny Sunday morning around this time of the year. I was working the 0900 London which is our first train South on a Sunday morning. We had just called at Milton Keynes and I was accelerating through Bletchley, we were bang on time, under green signals, beautiful blue skies and I was as usual loving my job. I glanced across to check my stops and schedule and as I looked up again there was a person with their back to me holding their arms out like a cross by the time I've processed what's happening (because it's so alien) I fully applied the brake and then I've hit the person; I heard the body rattling under the train. I hit the radio emergency call button to speak almost immediately to the controlling signaller, to report the incident and turn on the hazard warning lights to stop other trains. I prayed straight away for forgiveness for the person and that this would have no harmful effect on me, my health or the ability to do my job. I've seen the effects of these incidents on friends in the past and it has ruined their health and lives. One lovely gentleman I knew who post-incident was never himself after, and died of cancer within 18 months, previously having had excellent health."

(*Author's note. NB: This is an important point to take notice of; a relation between stress and cancer as Dr. Gabor Maté has demonstrated. See the end of my book for a quick signposting to his works.)

"The next thing a Manager from Network Rail shouted up to me and asked to come in the cab. This man (ex-forces) heard about the incident and ran around a mile and a half along the track to get to me. He was excellent. Also a lovely elderly lady a catering member of staff knew what had happened and made me a cuppa straight away and chatted briefly, the Train Manager also was supportive. Normal procedure is for a Driver Team Manager (DTM) to meet up with the Driver asap but incredibly the on-call DTM's son had a heart attack just after he got the call. I also spoke briefly to British Transport Police to ensure that there were no suspicious circumstances. Transport arrived and a Relief Driver and technical staff after around 1 hour 30 minutes and I walked away from the train without looking back. The NR Manager came with me, the limousine that was sent was going to take me home, but I just wanted to get the train home from Milton Keynes and so the NR chap drove me in his van from Bletchley his base. I got the train and that trains TM sat with me the whole way back to my depot, everyone was excellent, then the Station Team Leader waited until my taxi home arrived.

Post-incident my sleep was very disturbed with frequent flashbacks. I was going to return to work after one week but eventually couldn't because I was just exhausted through lack of sleep. My wife insisted I had counselling and my managers organised that for me. The counselling was excellent, and I returned to work 2 weeks post incident, my first trip accompanied by a DTM past the area concerned. Thankfully I didn't have to attend the coroner's court as this can be very traumatic too. It's a strange feeling when you consider that you've killed another person (however indirectly) but you make your peace with the situation the best way that you can. You always think maybe if I'd done this, that or whatever else, but then you think at the end of the day they don't know who you are who is driving, it's not personal, they're just so unbalanced that they use the train to end it all, so incredibly sad and in our job it's become almost an occupational hazard."

How on earth do you recover from such a shock?

Rescue me: cliff collapse

S recounts a time he was involved in a coastal rescue, where the predictable outcome was unavoidable. It still plays on his mind now.

"During a Coast Guard job in my first year as a Coast Guard rescue officer a fisherman was caught in a cliff collapse on a freezing cold snowy night. The fisherman was nowhere to be seen and it was our job to search the rescue area and rescue him as part of the cliff rescue team. On top of the cliff I was manning the main safety lines for our colleagues. The job went on for a few hours with the sad outcome of the fisherman being buried alive. This was a devastating discovery for the team, as we were unable to help as tonnes of rock were on top of him. All emergency services who attended knew that there was no way that anyone could survive such a terrible accident, so the search/ recovery was called off until daylight.

I returned home only to be kept awake with the thoughts like, *'What if he's still alive when we have returned home, and we could have saved him?'* The following day during the recovery it was made clear to the rescue team who had tirelessly worked the previous night, that there were many dangers that they had faced, but weren't aware of in the dark including the state of the cliff. It was looking like further cliff collapse was imminent; if the cliff had collapsed during the rescue attempt through the night it would have endangered the whole team.

 Post-incident, I experienced sleepless nights thinking about the events of that job and experiencing flashbacks. I would find myself having thoughts of sadness for the man involved and his family and friends, fear of what could have happened and anger of not doing more. This job being one in my first year as a Coast Guard rescue officer is one I always remember, and sometimes think about 13 years later."

Safely to the shore

Chris is a lifeboat service (RNLI) volunteer who offers support to the boat crews on the Cornish coast. Here's what he says about his role as a shore crew member.

"My experience is quite muted compared to the guys on the boat, who see events firsts first-hand. That being said, when we are on duty, and the outcome is not good, there is certainly an atmosphere in the boat house. Personally, I tend to have a quick pray when the boat is released onto the water, asking for God's grace and protection for those we are trying to aid. We had a good outcome last week with a local rescue – the boy was airlifted to hospital and made a full recovery, but the previous shout was a clear suicide attempt where the outcome was (bad). If someone is determined to end their life by throwing themselves onto rocks below, it invariably doesn't end well. Our guys use a process called TRiM: it's basically a procedure the RNLI use to help those affected mentally by traumatic events."

*TRiM is a confidential peer to peer programme to support people who have been exposed to such incidents and they are offered a meeting with a trained practitioner to talk through what happened and agree on any future support.

Behind bars

M worked in the prison service until he could hack it no longer. Here's what he said about this time of his life....

"I was 26 when I joined the Prison Service and after training, was sent to a Remand Centre in London. This catered for 16 to 21-year-olds. Inmates under punishment ate in their cell. I had been there about three months and was tasked with getting the trays put outside the cell for collection. One lad had hardly eaten anything I asked if he was OK to which he replied. "Yes, fine just not hungry". Just ten minutes later, the wing officer opened his cell to find him hanging. We quickly got him down and tried CPR to no avail. As the last to see him alive I had to give evidence at the inquest. It was emotional going through it in front of his family with them listening to the last moments of the seventeen-year-olds life. After the inquest, the lads father came up to me and said, "Thank you for doing what you could." I walked away thinking, "*Did I do all I could?*" Did we as a service do what we could? Everything was done to a time controlled, routine with few staff. I asked if he was OK, then accepted his reply... should I have asked again and got him to open up and spent some time talking to him? Probably yes, but at the time, the system would not allow for it. It stayed with me though for a long time, during which I became much better at reading people.

After my twelve-months' probation was over, I decided to specialise as a Hospital Officer, and trained at Charing Cross and Wormwood Scrubs Hospitals. I then got posted to Gloucester. Around this time The Thatcher Government decided that there was no such thing as mental illness, it was a personality disorder. So, they closed dozens of hospitals and sold them off for development. Bringing in 'Care in the Community', only they did not have the resources in place to provide it. Hence many of the people who had been in those hospitals, suddenly started to appear in prisons, who in themselves never had the resource or expertise to deal with them. This led to a spike in both suicides and assaults, both on staff and inmate to inmate. For some though, prison became a safe place, somewhere they had a bed, meals, and company. I recall two brothers that came in and out on a regular basis, it was Christmas, and they were looking forward to Christmas lunch at the prison, however one's sentence was coming to an end and because of Christmas and the weekend, his release was brought forward, and he was discharged on Christmas Eve. Four days later, they found his body on the bank of the River Severn.

While walking up into town, I saw an ambulance and the medics trying to talk to the person on the ground, I recognised him and tapped his leg and said, "John, speak to the medics." He opened one eye and said, "Go away *Mr. M*, I'm unconscious." These things made me angry, and I wrote a very well-received piece for the Prison Service Magazine and also to the Home Secretary. I was invited to a meeting in London, where a lot was said but there were no immediate changes. I transferred to Exeter, where with three local dedicated mental health units shut and turned into apartments, there was little difference. The answer seemed to be *Largactil* and *Kemadrin*. I met with the then Prisons Minister and she kept saying "I hear what you say...". Eventually, I snapped and said, "Stop hearing what I say and start f*****g well listening!" I then decided that I could no longer work in the Prison Hospital system. It was causing too much conflict within myself. So, I transferred back to being an officer, where there were some changes, and as acting Senior Officer on the remand wing, I did have time to talk and importantly listen. I will add it is 36 years since I left the hospital side and 25 years since I left the Prison service and there have been a lot of changes since then."

So there we go. That's an idea of what can happen to a man in uniform. I haven't even touched the sides here. So many more stories of course, from all over the world, but these ones above capture the essence of the subject I hope. The things a man sees, and experiences will stay with him and often trigger emotions decades later.

Chapter Eight

Family: Fathers, grandfathers, children

Having a family is an honour, a blessing and a legacy. No-one gives you a manuscript on how you do it; you just do it, with all your mistakes and triumphs bundled into one big package of fatherhood. Often, with all its business and pressure during the weekdays, the most amazing feeling can be simply sitting on the sofa together on a Saturday night, watching a film. The more experienced you are at being a father certainly does not mean you are better at it, although it would be nice to think so. I am a 'stepfather' first to two boys, and a 'natural' father to my own two. I am a husband, a lover, a brother and a son. Yet I still feel like a boy...

Sometimes a man can feel lonely, isolated and desperate, even when he is part of a large family, never physically alone. A man carrying his own worries whilst trying to take care of others, can feel overloaded, pressurized like a ticking time-bomb and exhausted in all his endeavours to keep his own boat afloat.

'Day to day, I just carried on reluctantly as I thought about my wife and young family back home, needing my presence. But I was caught between two worlds: I was committed to a job to pay the bills and all the money I owed, but I felt alone, in a no-man's land and, privately, my own mental health was on a knife edge. We men should really take our stresses seriously. Middle aged men run the highest risk of suicide. I barely confided in anyone, but sometimes I would lean against the door at 1L on the take-off run, and wonder what it might be like to operate the handle at the point of aircraft rotation and jump out. Thankfully, that remained a daydream and I carried on working for the airlines until I could finally do it no longer. I handed in my notice to my manager and breathed a sigh of relief. I was going home, but to quite what I didn't know....'

My mental health wasn't at an all-time high back then. Really I just didn't fancy the sensation of being sucked into a Rolls Royce Trent engine and being chewed up by fan blades, along with putting 300 lives at risk. I didn't ever want to do it. My family needed me by far the most. My friends needed me. Possibly even the world needed me. That was the bigger picture.

Extremes

There has always been a part of me that likes my own company, despite being gregarious and outwardly sociable. I like the quiet and solitude of driving alone, yet I also loved the euphoria of being on stage as a rock drummer with my bandmates as the audience sang our songs back to us. I appreciate the peace of the dawn and the explosion of colours that only an early sunrise can paint. I like the feeling of pressing 'send' on a completed work-report, as well as a complete burst of serotonin-energy on my bicycle. I relish the danger of the surf crashing over me in the Cornish sea pulling me under, but equally the calm surrender of the sunset to the evening, as I walk from the shores back to camp, treading the soft sand underfoot, with my wife's hand in mine. Call it the complexity of being a human, but I just like extremes.

Extremes. You'll certainly get those as a father, a husband and a family member. Some of the things I struggle with include: my role and placing in the family, my virility, my ageing, why I feel I lack authority, feeling like a peacekeeper and a compromiser and how I fit into all of it. It's a daily walk I take with all of these factors, and what I do with all of it.

Snapped

It was a Sunday morning just a few years ago and I had taken all that I could. I stopped the car at the side of the road and walked away from everyone, leaving the driver's door ajar. I couldn't take anymore. My head felt like it was about to combust. I kept walking and didn't look back. I had snapped. I was to keep walking for another three hours heading home. I didn't know what I was going to do. I had gone way past caring. There was no money in my pocket, no joy in my pounding heart, just the clothes on me. I thought about how easy it would be to rip the SIM card out of my phone, throw it into a ditch, and walk until I dropped, if necessary to the other side of England. I worked out how no-one would ever find me again, as I would blend into streets, alleyways and seaports. I walked under bridges, through open countryside and along country roads which actually did take me home. All the way there I thought about how rubbish I must be and how unwanted I was. It took those three hours for me to process and eventually decide to calm down. I know what it is to snap. Yet I also know how much can actually be resolved by sitting down and talking. I decided to try again and fight another day.

Getting older

The passage from younger man with limited responsibilities, into middle age and the point of no return is a strange one. The truth is that we all go through *seasons*. With it, I have not found myself yearning for what's past, but trying to fathom what may lie ahead. *What will I look like? Will I lose my hair? What if I get prostate cancer? Will I still be employable? What could I turn my hands to next? Will I be a grandparent? What if I lose everything? What if I end up alone?* These are very real fears and I am sure I am not the only one to ask myself these questions. When you get older, you also come to understand as a man that your body is in mild decline and perhaps your physical needs are too. I can feel my body changing like someone threw a switch at age 50. (Apparently I don't look 50, but there are days when I certainly feel it.)

If you have children, they will always come first, even though we might find that hurtful. Our first thoughts could be defensive: *'Then why am I needed? What is my purpose here? What am I in relation to the family?* Men can find themselves slightly lost in the whole equation of a family where usually it starts with two people. I have pondered this question of *what I actually am in the family*, if the kids come first, even at their 'coming of age'. I have reconciled this in my head within about eight minutes; I have no idea about the symbiotic relationship between a mother and her child which she has pushed out of her body and nurtured over the early years and beyond. I will however respect it, as I too was pushed out of my own mum's body and nurtured similarly to make me into the eventual man I have become. (Please, don't comment.)

The messiness of families: Hamlet

When I look back at how much ground I have covered, how many battles I have fought, how many mini-triumphs and how many mountains I have climbed since having a family, then it really awakens me into seeing it as a journey where I am not the only character, but maybe like *Hamlet*, just the main *protagonist*. (That much I remember from my English Literature lessons at school.) You see, Hamlet's dad was murdered by his uncle. His girlfriend drowns herself. Then at the other end of the scale you get semi-comic characters like *Rozencrantz and Guildenstern*. It all ends in catastrophe with a blood bath in the royal household. That's Shakespeare's take on family apparently. Messy. Yet for all its messiness, family and fatherhood is a wonderful idea. Even though it looks and feels at times like it barely works for us men, we are the central characters. So much relies on us protagonists to be strong, solid and safe. In other words, less *Frank Spencer* and more *Bruce Willis*. More Brut than Demi-sec. (Ahem.)

Breaking away

I can offer this next truth to those of you thinking of getting married. You will have to decide to actively separate from your blood-family to make the choice to be with another. You then create your own off-shoot from there. Kids may or may not follow. I can speak from experience that leaving my original family to make a life of my own was a hard experience as my own parents' partialities, preconceptions and prejudices forced my hand to my determination to be with the one I love. My parents made their feelings clear and they were wrong. They showed their colours when I announced our engagement by leaving the room immediately. They couldn't have been colder. So, I blocked them out of the planning and carried on as if they were not there. Was that hard? Of course. When they could see it was full steam ahead, they decided at the final hour to come onboard or face being left at the platform. It made me feel more of a man for going through this threshold and fighting for what I want. So, if you're contemplating getting married, you may want to prepare yourself for a fight. (Staying married also requires a fight.)

Infertility, impotence and prematurity.....

You're a man. With it comes responsibilities, demands and urges. What if you can't for whatever reason *perform?* What if the sexual side of things doesn't measure up (deliberate choice of words), and you don't quite hit the mark? It can be devastating for both of you. It can make you feel like you're not truly a man. It can make your woman feel like she's missing out, or at worst, used. That can really drive a wedge between couples. I really don't write this lightly I can assure you. In fact, it makes me feel really uncomfortable... I am a sensual being as well as 'a nice guy'. I have passion and a glint in my eye when I am up for it, but equally I tend to get over-excited. I wish I was less *Panasonic*, and more *Duracell*. What about if you're eager for physical relations but your partner doesn't find you sexually attractive anymore? You could always suggest meeting in the middle. (Ahem.)

I have always taken it for granted that my sperm are healthy, and I have brought two beautiful children into the world with more than a little help from my wife. But what does it feel like for a man who cannot do the same?

Crying at the traffic lights

Finding out that you cannot have kids must be heart-wrenching. My friend went through just that. The clinics, IVF and all that was associated with it. His only daughter was the product of that, and he describes her as 'a miracle baby'. He gave me an insight into the emotional rollercoaster and damage that can happen. He called it 'crying at the traffic lights.' That's all he needed to say. Despite their joy at having a baby against all the odds, spending a lifetime raising their family, he and his wife split after 23 years of marriage. He asks himself now; "How is that possible??" He still gets emotional just thinking about it and has had many a time finding himself racing around doing normal life, then stopping briefly only to find that through tears, the past has caught up with him.

He's right. How after a myriad of time together can it be time to call it a day on a lifetime's commitment?

Us men feel like we have to hold it together, but sometimes we know that deep fear inside that we are just little boys pretending, not real men. We want to be warriors, we want to be brave, but we are weary of the battlefield, ill-equipped and insufficient. If we fail, we fear that we can be retired from the front-line. Replaced easily. There are always newer models to upgrade to. We fear that we might actually be no more important than a disposable razor. This feeds into the wound I carry. That I am insufficient, not quite a real man and somewhere inside, still that little boy being shamed in front of everyone.

If I have relationship ups/downs from time to time, it's hard not to feel alone. Just from living my life, I understand if only from the personal lives of people I know that this is common. It doesn't make it easier; it just means that it happens to pretty much everyone, and there would probably be something abnormal if all was dandy the whole time. I often feel a genuine tear come to my eye if I hear about people I know splitting up, giving up on years of marriage and lives together. I hear of couples who have spent years bringing up a child or children, and then calling it a day as they lost themselves in the whirlwind, when they're left to face each other alone. All that sacrifice, losing yourselves, your initial romance and your spark to create a family and then...? It really affects me personally. Maybe it's because I realise that all relationships are tender, and it could so easily happen to me, unless

I work hard at mine. I don't want to be someone who gives up at the slightest hurdle. I want to be an *overcomer*, I really do. I am learning that if you have a problem, you should do your best to repair it quickly. Flowers are a gesture that can help but communication is better. Flora I have found, leads to suspicious questioning. (*"What have you done?!"*) Chocolate is an excellent substitute, but it has to be either expensive-looking or weigh at least 500g. Even then, it may or may not work, and that's just the price you pay. (Sometimes, my debit card could do a lot more than I allow it.)

I have tried to imagine what life looks like for men who find themselves alone after a long relationship. With the loss of such, do you put yourself back years into the place you were had the relationship not started? (Sorry that's my legal mind working; remedies.) Do you automatically wipe out everything as though starting again? Is there a period of loss and mourning? (There surely has to be.) Do you regress to believing that you are the same person as you were at the start of it all? Does it really all feel like it counted for nothing, or do you take comfort that in that time you have grown and changed? Do you feel it has been time wasted, or that you have failed? Do you feel empty, in despair or philosophical? Do you feel that your life is over, that you are unlovable or that you are free? *Can I ever love or be loved again?* From what I know and what I suspect, all of these feelings will wash over a man. In those moments we need time to face our pain, embrace our inner turmoil and cry it out. Tears are healing and so is time.

'Kev the spray'

About 17 years ago, 'Kev the spray' did a sterling job of powder-coating my pearlescent white fuel tank into black gloss so that it would convert the whole Yamaha 750cc big trailie into a mean dark monster. (I only do black motorbikes. Silver is ok.) As he drank a mug of tea at Gav's table, he smiled as he told us how his *'ex-Mrs.'* got the shock of her life as a result of her actions. Not only had she been cheating on him, moved her new lover in and kicked Kev out, but had also left him with CCJs (County Court Judgement) and loan repayments for household items she was enjoying with her new man. In a blind rage, Kev, after realising this, simply drove his van into the side of the house. It might have cost him more, but he certainly felt better. He was laughing about it in retrospect, so I figured he deserved the whole packet of custard creams for that story alone. He lived to fight another spray.

Coming out?

I have a friend who, like me, is besotted by aircraft and has just scored his pilot's licence (PPL). We used to work together at an airport for a while and stayed in touch. He has always been a really lovely chap, polite, softly spoken and a pleasure to talk with; he's also a musician. I love Boeing, while he prefers Airbus, but we don't fight about it anymore. We still keep in touch and on one of his visits to see me before the 2020 lockdown, he told me about the news he had; there was something he had wanted to tell his parents, something that he had struggled with inside for years, until the pressure had become too great to bear. He came out. He broke down in tears of absolute relief, when they said they always thought he might be, and he was still accepted. But not by me. (He's an Airbus fan, but I'm a Boeing man. How can there ever be reconciliation?) Only joking, he's alright... for an A330.

Your father

"Your Father?!" The words my mother would sometimes deliver in complete exasperation at her choice of husband. There was something quite normal, comforting yet deeply amusing about the arguments they used to have, and the best ones were always in the kitchen for some reason. I appreciate this is well-known, but guys, like it or not, it's your own dad who gives you the main blueprint for how you'll be in this world. So, for all his faults, I decided to cut my dad a little slack and try to imagine what his upbringing must have been like, extending it

from his own father and to his grandfather. Just that simple act of imagination can provide the background to why things are as they are for us men now.

My parents owned a majestic-looking house in the latter part of their career as caterers turned hoteliers. Pouring everything into their businesses, they grew them throughout the late sixties until the early eighties until they felt a change was on the horizon and a new opportunity lay before them. It was a risk, but they had sold all their property in a prime city centre location to pour everything into this new venture, a luxurious hotel uniquely placed close enough to town, yet far away enough to give the feeling of the countryside. It could have worked brilliantly, had it not been for the bombing of a U.S. passenger plane and a war in the Middle East. Those two events practically killed off American tourism long enough for the bank to threaten to repossess unless they sold up double-quick. I was aware of what was going on, but unless you're personally affected, then you won't truly understand, and my folks did a good job of shielding me from their stress. I saw my dad sit on the same sofa for years in that house, becoming more and more tired, and physically larger and larger. We would do all of the gardening between us and to get it into perspective, just my part of the mowing would take four hours alone. I was in my teens then and helping my dad was part of my duty as well as pulling my weight in the house. Sometimes we would take a break to sit down and have a can of *Carlsberg* together in the sun, and I sensed this gave him pleasure as a dad. Those moments brought us a little closer. Father and son. We worked hard and it's never escaped me how hard my parents both worked. (If my dad wasn't sitting on that sofa, he found another one when the folks ran a boutique together. He used to read the local paper there, occasionally winking at me whilst trying to pretend he was holding down a conversation with one of the elderly ladies who used to visit the shop.) However, I too am working hard doing completely different things to them, almost as if to say *"I'm not going to follow your blueprint; I'm making my own path..."* Deliberately, I often try new avenues, if only because I have that image in my mind of my dad sitting alone now, in his chair, struggling with his weight and close to giving up. It's my warning sign. I still have vigour, energy and determination in me. And a cheap skipping rope I bought from a charity shop which I sometimes pull out if I can see my girth expanding.

Fatherhood

Before I start: I love all four of my children. I'm deeply proud of all of them, for who they are, where they are heading and what they are achieving. One day they will be fathers. Except for my daughter obviously, but sometimes I do wonder...Over the years, it's dawned on me that fatherhood is not for everyone. As I look around, I can see that it is easier by far to *make* a child, than to bring one up with love, discipline, protection and correction. Parenting has never come easy to me, apart from the play-bit. I didn't want the same blueprint of parenting that had been handed down to me, so I tried to be myself, but it's hard to entirely shake the past. There were so many things my folks got right, yet it was usually their way or the highway. I was mostly compliant, unlike my sister who drove my folks so mad, she got sent to a school far away....

I have to say that becoming a father and sticking through thick and thin has added several other dimensions to my life. Before children, I could do what I pleased. Once in the water, I was in for the ride. It won't end for me now as I'll always be 'Dad' or 'Simon', and for all the hard bits, there are many more amusing ones to counteract them. Daily, it's the petty arguments, the door-slamming and the 'Where's my socks?!' shouting from upstairs. That's just me. The kids are far worse. But they keep me on my toes and, there's a mini sense of achievement just to get them out of the door and into the car to get to school on time and back.

The thing that I have never quite got right is the discipline side, as I'm either too soft or too harsh. I think my children all feel loved in their own way, and I try to treat them as individuals, understanding that they respond to slightly different things. (Chocolate or sweets, however, are the universal medium for bargaining. They even steal them from my bedroom, so I have to be very clever with new hiding-places which often render the treats out of date or inedible. Lately, they've got so desperate, they even go for the cooking chocolate. Reminds me of what my mum used to moan about.) If they break a plate or spill food on the floor by accident, they don't tend to apologise or properly clean it up. These are small things but maybe I have found myself being too precious with some things, and too relaxed about others. I blame the parents. (Ahem.) Don't get me wrong, but kids know which buttons to press to get their own way, and they know very well how to be divisive. They will always try to get what they want by playing one parent off the other, and sometimes it works. What they're not so hot on is realising one sublime thing: *Us dads are ahead of them. We were kids once and we know all the tricks better than them.* I have also learned the trick of not entering every argument they present before me, no matter how tempting. I have figured that especially when my teenagers feel that they have succeeded in 'winning' an argument, bringing in ridicule and rudeness, that it won't be long before they enter adulthood and, just like me as a late teenager, they'll suddenly be confronted with the truth: *how little they actually know.* I don't need revenge. It's not my style. It'll come back on them later down the line. Petrol is expensive, council tax hurts and rent will swallow up most of what they thought was disposable income. I am really trying to suppress the wry smile that is forming. *Who's the clever one now?*

The incredible parts of fatherhood for me are the following:

I am bringing up all four of my kids into a Judeo-Christian walk to respect others, forgive, show mercy, be kind, show love and not favouritism, help those who feel weak and do their best. I invent my steps most days with fatherhood. Am I succeeding? Most days, I feel like I'm not, but I still keep trying. On the balance of probabilities, I am winning...just.

Step-parenting

This is a subject that has been so widely written about and commented on that anything from me would seem to be superfluous. I will add something though and it's a military analogy. Although it works well, it's sometimes tough, and it can be supremely difficult as often you'll feel stuck in a no-man's land. Solitary, outgunned and sometimes in an impossible situation, feeling like 'the enemy', when all you're trying to do is the right thing. It's no exercise. It's the real thing. Something that has stuck with me recently though is to think about what it must be like for the 'biological father;' to see someone else looking after his kids, and possibly even doing a better job than himself? That would eat me up, but then again, as I have said, parenting is not for everyone. Pass me a *Thunder-flash*, I'm going in....

Other writers have the proven theories, but I will give you my reality. I have invested time, love and energy into raising kids who aren't strictly speaking my own. I've pushed them on the swings, chased them in the park, taken them to and from various activities, fed them, wiped their tears, put them to bed and overall loved them as my own. They are my life. Some of you will be thinking; *"So what?"* Others might be thinking; *"I couldn't do that."* No matter, it's just where my path led me and I'm grateful for the opportunity to be tested as worthy, and it has been hard particularly in the teenage years. I have also not been given a straightforward run for my money, with 'biological dad' still on the scene. We do get along quite well, but both of us have our moments. In the main though, even if we disagree on some things, it doesn't last long, and we understand that it's the boys who need to be put ahead of everything. I have a blended family and mostly it works. I can say that any parenting can be hard, whether they're your own kids or otherwise.

Clashes

My own mental health has been severely tested as I have clashed on occasion and have had to back down, trying to reconcile 'being head of the household' with something we call 'love'. I think, somewhat reluctantly, that 'choosing your battles' is a good strategy, as it's pointless to 'win' every argument and end up shaking with anger. I've found that when you have a strong-willed child, by experience of this not working, you don't go head to head, but you find a different way to approach it. I have had clashes physically before and it certainly ain't pretty. I know I'm not the only one. If I add fuel to the fire of an argument by getting fired up myself, it increases the intensity of the moment and can lead me to saying things I later regret or acting in an over-emotional way that just isn't *me*.

What I am trying to say is this: I am not naturally argumentative, nor do I have to be right about everything. If I clash with any of my kids who are inclined that way, I have found it a better tactic to not give them any fuel to continue an argument. In other words, I shut my mouth and choose my words carefully. It's not quite the same as backing down, but it's realising that my health is important too and I am not going to raise my own blood pressure just for others' entertainment. This is not how my own parents would have acted, but this is what is going to preserve my own mental outlook. I don't *have* to win an argument with my children; any of them. It's worthwhile remembering that once they enter adulthood, they will certainly have enough problems ahead, which they will really have to work ways through. It's better sometimes to be quiet. Always watch the quiet ones.

A model father

I have a very good friend, again someone I don't talk with too often, but when we do, as with all the best friendships, we can carry on exactly where we last left off with no fuss. He and I are both semi-pro musicians and have a shared love of the *English Electric Lightning*. If you know what I'm talking about, I don't need to say anything else, you'll understand completely. He's so eloquent when he texts me, it makes me embarrassed to call myself a writer. I sometimes wonder how he still faces each day and stands in the face of what life throws at him. He has gone through a marital breakdown, recent death of his mother, his father died when he was 30 years-old and his daughter is wayward. That last bit is the one which hurts the most. He has no idea where she is most of the time. He is always on edge for a phone call from the police, a sighting in a different town hundreds of miles away, no connection on her mobile number, fearing the worst or a panic call begging him to pick her up from a distant city with a wad of money. She had an eating disorder which hospitalised her a few years ago and she was under watch. I have seen the photos of her; she's a beautiful girl and her parents are balanced. He has aged inside and out because of worry for her. That's without the last year of lockdown completely decimating his normal income sources. What do you think he might feel from time to time, should he drink too much *Glenfiddich* and start to feel sorry for himself? Life happens and it's how you deal with it. He's an overcomer just for getting up and facing the world each morning. I phoned him today. All I had to do was mention Lightning F6 models and he was in much better spirits. It must be the distinctive nose-cone. Here's what he texted me...

"With models we can generate fashion and own these shapes that captivate our imagination. We can lose ourselves to our obsessive nature. Get lost in the sensory delights of opening and unwrapping. Rest in the trusted authority of the instructions. The evocative smells of glue and paint. A real fighter jet is brilliant but close in is too big to be fully appreciated for its overall shape awesomeness. They look better from a bit of a distance. You can hold the model. See it from every angle close in. Employ the imagination. Find the creator in the detail as well as the devil. I did it a second time in life after dad died cos planes were our thing. Did loads as a kid. At every level it was a shared obsessive passion. It was just one of the things I did as a child.

Then as an adult at the time mid 30's. (Not really an adult at all). On losing Dad quite early, I wasn't ready to let him go. So I suddenly got right back into it. Because they come in bits and end up whole, it feeds and nourishes an inner hope. A positive creative artistic expression. There is a lovely sense of accomplishment holding your favourite shape in the world. Having been part of its becoming. There's definitely a zen vibe of calm meditative contemplation. One can possess a version of the form that captivates. That symmetry that can soar and roar roll and turn. Climb and dive. Applying pressure to its graceful equilibrium.

I don't do 'em now. I've let Dad go mostly. I still look up every time I hear an engine in the sky and remember the smile on my Dads face when I was very tiny. I pointed up and said (of a unique and beautiful expose of such symmetry and noisy grace); "Look Dad, a VC10." I loved the shape and realised I was connected to Dad like I wanted to be. Silly little model aeroplanes. Helped me fashion and hold my sadness and loss and gave me an outlet for my grief. And captivated once more my boyish obsessive nature."

Wow. I'm honestly lost for words here. When you see the things which others deal with, your perspective is straightened out, your attitude is checked, your heading is stabilised. I promise I'm not trying to stall you.

Loneliness within a family

It is possible to feel isolated even when surrounded by loved ones. Arguments are normal in a family, especially a large one. Disagreement is normal and everyone wants to have their voice. I think I'm pretty balanced, but that's just my view. As I have said, my downside is that I'm sometimes too playful and often too sensitive. Sometimes, I have found that being backed into a corner can make me say things I don't mean, causing unnecessary damage and hurt to others. Time to go for a walk. It's actually when I *step back* from the heat of an argument that can only rage like a wildfire and destroy what I've taken precious time to build, that I can process the problem properly. It's nearly always something I can recover from if I just don't *over-react*. Even if it takes a couple of hours of quiet time with myself by retreating into my 'cave', I have found that this is vital to restoration. Many an argument has been needlessly fanned into flame by a sharp unbridled tongue. Remembering that as children, we take into life those curses, hurtful words and shameful moments we have experienced, it's far more noble a thing to show restraint. In other words, just because you have a gun, it doesn't mean you should fire it.

I had a largely happy upbringing, son to a hardworking 'catering-couple' who did their best to bring us up respecting others, being polite and always eating up all our food because "there are children starving in Africa." I was fortunate because I had the love of two parents to guide me and provide for me. For so many men, this has not been the case.

A father's wound

L was a former bandmate, a likeable rogue who had an incredible singing and production talent. His finest moments were when he had a band around him to temper some of his more fanciful leanings, as democracy can bring balance. He had some truly great ideas, some of which were innovative and so we followed through as a band on a few of them. He had so much going for him, but about nine years ago, I felt the strongest inner sense to change my path away from him, and our paths diverged. Out of the blue, I found out that he was headed for prison because of a drugs-bust; he was producing on an outrageous scale (football pitch size) below ground. Ironically, he didn't even smoke or drink. Apparently, the Crown Court judge really wanted to make an example of him to others who wanted to 'get rich quick' through drugs-production, with a much longer sentence than he eventually received. I don't know what being incarcerated has taught him, as on the handful of occasions I have since talked to him by phone, it seems obvious that he might carry on where he left off. Not exactly in the same *way*, but in the sense that he will be out for himself and what he can take from the world. He will certainly reinvent himself and acclimatize to his surroundings, before starting on another equally daring exercise which will involve self-promotion, risk and almost certainly fame... or notoriety. I almost envy him for his audacious outlook, but I can trace this back to one key thing. His father died when he was eight years old and consequently, he had not that hand upon his shoulder to guide him, to show him how to be a man and crucially, to love him. This was pointed out to him by a girl he had two-timed, and he took it badly, like a direct uncaring wound to his heart shouting; "How dare she say that!" It was actually the most poignant and accurate arrow he had ever received.

It made me ponder all those celebrity interviews I have read over the years. You know the ones: where the person has had a poor or adverse start in life and vowed he or she would never allow themselves to be in that position ever again. The money and the fame would put everything right of course. What I have found is that circumstances may change, but the *essence of that person's character* remains, for better or for worse. He wrote a song that we used to play in our band's early days. I didn't like it at first, but it grew on me over time. Unusually, it wasn't about a girl, breaking up or sex. It was about growing up, losing his dad when he needed him the most, being fearful of going to senior school, happy days throwing frisbee in the park and yet a yearning for his father to be there to see him all grown up. The song grew on me as I would lose myself in it on stage. It resolved like this....

"All the memories I have of you are short and sweet and very few,
- that's why it's easy to cry...
I wish that I had one more day, I have so much I have to say, but hey-
It's too late for that now...
And so, do you look down on me? I hope to God that you can see,
That you are now a part of me....and see me for all I am....
Where did you go...?" ('Blotting Paper', written 1999)
This might be the deepest question a man asks when he has lost the father he loves and needs: 'Where did you go?'

Justice in action, but where was dad?

There comes a time in your life when someone will cross the line and try to push you around. In this next story, I stood up against an aggressor because it felt like the right thing to do. It's not very often in my life that I have to stand up in front of others and stand my ground. But it got me thinking as I processed it for several months after.....

I was cycling through town after finishing my day job, heading out on my drum-teaching rounds. Down a side street, a small black cabriolet BMW deliberately hurtled past me way too close for any comfort and oblivious to the 20mph signs. I recognised it, having seen it race down the same street on several other occasions, at double the speed limit. I carried on cycling and got to the main road intersection where I found that car selfishly blocking the road past the traffic lights. I cycled past and did my usual 'lifesaver look' over my shoulder which made me wonder if he might take this personally. Well, he did, and a few seconds later as he accelerated past me he went to nudge me off the road with a quick sharp left-hand wheel turn which nearly sent me toppling into the kerb. Furiously I pedalled and almost caught up with him ahead, when without warning he slammed on his brakes in the middle of the road leaving me to skid to a halt. He flung open his door and jumped out of the car just like an episode of 'NYPD Blues' leaving his two homies inside. "What the f*** do you think you're doing??!!" he shouted at me. (All I wanted to do was say my peace.)

Approaching me obviously full of testosterone and like he was on the set of a budget rap video (and believe me, I know what budget looks like), he turned it all on *me*. A barrage of personal insults and physical threats were spat vitriolically at me in those few moments down a metaphorical mic: *to decapitate me, run me down and kill me* (not in that order) if he ever saw me again, except less-politely, until I squared right up to this horrible guy, aware that bus-drivers, lorry-drivers, van-drivers and car-drivers were all around watching in their queues. His arms flailed wildly when I invaded his personal space at that moment, but our man was very careful, despite his threats, not to lay a finger on me. Still I stood, impervious to his temper, because I had suffered bullies before, had endured hardships of various kinds (including private schooling) and been to global warzones, whilst this kid was sucking his thumb. This was *my* city too. (Yes, he could have had a knife, but I had a *Zefal* bicycle pump.) He even dared to call me "old man". I wagged my finger at him, aware he had clocked my greying hair under my stickered skate-helmet and simply said with a sly smirk; *"I was young once..."*

Off he finally sped, up familiar turn-offs to probably inflict misery on anyone else daring to use the same adopted roads. A van driver mouthed at me as I got back on my bike, "You OK?" I nodded. I reported the incident a couple of hours later and then forgot about it, as apparently, I should have reported it at the time and there was nothing further the police could do. A few days later I saw a police car down the original street, as I was parking up and it turned out that of all the PCs I could have approached, she was in charge of my case. There was very little to go on as the number plate info I gave produced no matches. We kept in touch. Then the best and most unlikely sequence of things happened over the course of a week...

I was driving between visits to my clients and saw our man, quite by accident, with a blonde girlfriend and possibly their baby girl, outside a flat down a street in a suburb close to home. I watched thinking what you're probably thinking; *How can he be a daddy?* A couple of days later, I was driving in the same area (I get around) and found myself driving right behind him. I backed off a little and phoned the police straight away. Their advice was not to get too near. I passed the number plate over the phone and then turned off. There was something sneaky, subversive and detective-like about this. (The perpetrator had only ever seen me on a bicycle and didn't know I owned an MPV, which towered above his little run-around. Mine could fit a wife, myself, four kids, 2 bicycles and a weekly shop. It could tow a 5-berth caravan. It was also black, like a secret service vehicle. Follow that.)

The next day, I happened to be cycling along a canal path when I saw him and his family coming. I kept going and was aware that although he recognised me as we all passed within a hair's-breadth, he kept his head down and wasn't going to make a scene near his girlfriend and the pushchair. The final clincher was that I saw his car again in town and finally made sense of the puzzle. His front and rear number plates didn't match. *They were faked.* With that info I passed on my witness statement to another officer and waited. It wasn't to be long... Apparently, he had been physically and verbally threatening to a lady on the same day, but in a supreme twist, she was wearing a body-cam and had filmed the entire episode. With the combination of evidence from the pair of us, the Crown Prosecution Service pushed the case forward as there was a reasonable prospect of conviction. I found out that he was just given a rap (sic) on the knuckles and a final warning in court. I had to leave it behind me.

A few months later, I thought I would email the original PC who had been my case officer. This was her news; "He was given a warning but then he got arrested again and was in court for the same offence and was sent down for two years... a result." My initial sense of triumph was short-lived as I felt for my enemy, and was quickly replaced by two sombre questions I asked myself:

'How can a young guy become so angry, that it overflows onto complete strangers? Was it the absence of a dad that's made him so aggressive with so much to prove?'

Absent fathers

About ten years ago, I used to volunteer at a youth prison, with a handful of the musicians and a GP from a church we attended. I was on the monthly rota and did a handful of these visits which highlighted to me how fortunate I actually was in my life for so many reasons. Through security, down corridors, the sounds of doors being unlocked and then slammed behind you again before being led into the chapel to set up your gear for the morning service. Outside was the *AstroTurf* football ground, with young men kicking the balls around before being assembled for the service. In came the inmates around 09.45, sitting in rows of chairs, some goofing with their friends, others sat quietly contemplative, with guards of both sexes standing behind them watching, occasionally smiling. There was a kind of a bond between custody officers and prisoners. I knew a guard there who showed me among other objects, her sharp blade on her utility belt (although she was nothing like *Batman*). She explained that it was for cutting people down if they were found suspended in their cells. She had been forced to use it twice. As she told me about her job it was with a heavy heart that she explained one key unifying reason why so many young men were in jails like these: "Simon, just about every single lad is in here because they didn't have a dad to guide them into making good choices, show them love and what it is to be a man."

I looked online and realised this is not isolated. If you were the devil and you wanted to bring mankind down, what better way to do it than to attack fatherhood? Get the head and the rest should tumble. Talking of *Batman*, was it not the young man *Bruce Wayne* who was brought up under the guidance of a trusted male role model, his butler/ guardian *Alfred*? I'm not saying everyone should have a butler, but we all need an 'Alfred', a trusted male, an advisor who can give counsel, moral support and even wisdom. If you don't have a dad, if he is absent, or even if he is long gone, then an Alfred might be just the kind of man who can stand in that gap. More like an eagle than a Penguin.

When I was younger, absenteeism was frowned upon. Now it's unchecked. All too often, young men have their fun and then run off leaving the woman to bear the consequences. Children are often raised single-handedly, without enough support (maintenance, presence and guidance) and then are introduced to a world, missing something. The cycle often continues. I know that's an easy summary and it's a generalisation but it's from some of the experiences which I have seen that I write. I'll balance it. There are plenty of guys around who will do the right thing and be a strong presence for children. Play, eat, read with them. Go out for walks, skim stones and climb trees with them. Treat others well. Stand up for injustice, be it an elderly man being bullied, or signing a petition for a worthy cause. Use their reasoning to stop fights, rather than their fists. You could call them knights, but they are just men doing what they were supposed to do all along. In chainmail.

Be like a father to someone

I feel a little self-conscious relating this story but it kind of makes sense here. I was sitting at my desk in the catering office about 13 years ago, when in walked one of my younger staff members, a well-built Polish guy, wearing a baseball cap and bulky jacket. I looked up instinctively to say hello but was shocked to see his face heavily bruised with two black eyes and visible swelling. I got him to sit down and tell me what had happened. His 'crime' was to have been walking down a street in a suburb of the city, talking Polish to his girlfriend. That's it. For that, he was jumped by three English guys who beat him senseless. He was able to handle himself but was overpowered, while his girlfriend watched helplessly. I was incensed as I shared what had happened with a nurse, angered by the injustice and how I felt like writing to the local paper. She said, "It's up to *you* to tell people; you're the only one." The letter I wrote to the paper was published a few days later with the bold title *'Ashamed to call myself English...'* (paraphrased). It didn't change the world. It didn't get my friend justice. It didn't get his assailants locked up. What it did do was more subtle. I put myself in his position and thought about what it would feel like to be in a foreign country and be treated like that but with no-one caring. I think he thanked me for standing up to voice what had happened. I wasn't like his father at all, but maybe for a second I was. Sometimes you have to stand up and be counted. The pen can be mightier than the sword, but I would have had more pleasure acting like Charles Bronson. Without the 'tache.

Grandfathers

What is it about grandfathers that we younger men yearn for? Is it the stability and wisdom of a life gone by shown in the lines on their faces, and the lessons learned that deep inside we crave, as we stumble on our own life's course? Or is it simply that they wear warm jumpers, comfortable slacks and sensible shoes? There is something deep inside of me that would have loved to have known the steadying hand of my father's father on my shoulder, with that familiar glint in his eyes.

I never got to know my two grandads properly as I was but a baby. My grandad on my father's side I only knew as *'Nonno'* (Italian for *grandpa*) and there was something honourable about him, which I always detect when my dad talks about him. He was a proud yet fairly quiet man who was a foreman in a factory throughout the forties, fifties and sixties, having brought up no less than seven children during the poverty of the Second World War years in the north of Italy. For that alone, I should congratulate him. He had a strong moral sense of right and wrong and was apparently well-respected in the community. (Italians love that word *'respect'*. You see it mentioned in all the Mafia films.) Apparently, he held me tight and lovingly as a baby through proud tears, before he eventually passed away. I never got to learn how to fish with him, learn Italian or have him read to me until I fell asleep in his arms, as he died when I was still barely an infant. Nonno was all the good bits of *Don Corleone* as portrayed by *Marlon Brando*. I sometimes wonder if I have any of his character inside me. (Nonno's, not Marlon's.)

Contrast this with my English mother's father. My two grandfathers were very different, and it was my aunt who filled in all the lacking details as to why a young man with so much promise and talent could end up taking a path of deviousness and malevolence. He had been brought up in the war years as a part of a large family so you can see instant parallels. Owing to his own father's quest for fairness, he was denied an education at a nominal cost which was offered to him by a 'grammar school'. He had been identified as an outstanding scholar and was offered the opportunity to study there, but his own father had refused as 'what he did for one, he would have to do for the others too'. A little like Antonio Salieri (the villain in *'Amadeus'*), my English grandfather became bitter over time and apparently became a liar, a cheat, a gambler and a womanizer. He was booted out of the Air Force for forgery. He was aggressive to his own daughters. He would beat his wife throughout her life, before eventually finishing her off in hospital, but not before forging her will. One of the witnesses was not even in the country at the purported time of the 'signing'. That much was certainly proven. The detectives worked hard to prosecute him over the course of two years, having to investigate every new false trail he would lead them down, and my folks even ended up in The Royal Courts of Justice or *The Old Bailey* as it was known. (I just found out from my dad that the case was brought in front of the same high court judge who had presided over the inquest into the death of Princess Diana.) My grandfather was to end up dying at home of natural causes, having led a life of deception, coercion and battery. I was never to properly know him at all. (Stop looking at me like that.)

It actually pains me to write this as it seems there was nothing positive about that grandfather. The problem is that he wasn't just the sum of the things he *did*. He was obviously broken inside, and as the saying goes, '*hurt-people hurt people.*' I would hope that if I am ever blessed enough to be a grandpa, that I might give some wisdom, tenderness and love back to those little ones. More importantly, frighten the life out of them with some of the most elaborate chase-games mankind has ever witnessed. In sensible shoes of course.

Like a grandfather...

Every now and then you meet a man at peace with himself, who has obviously made mistakes, yet has emerged repentant and wiser. *R* was a gentle man in his mid-eighties, loyal, frail and in need of help with the everyday tasks he used to be able to do. I would take him shopping every Thursday afternoon and he used to tell me it meant the world to him, more than I could ever realise. He was prone to losing his balance and was to be a frequent visitor to the local 'falls clinic' at the city's hospital. He loved *Sinatra, Elvis* and fifties rock 'n' roll. There was something about him that I felt drawn to. He was a victim of fraudsters and I taught him how to handle phone calls like that, and he felt empowered to tackle their deceitful methods. He may have been elderly, but he was definitely perceptive, and could tell who was true and who was fiendish. (When a new tenant came on the scene to occupy the flat upstairs, and within days started a subtle campaign to intimidate and unnerve the younger couple who had problems of their own downstairs, *R* saw straight through it immediately as he noted her tone and a funny look in her eye. She wasn't to be trusted.) He had a family once, but he didn't like to talk about it and buried it saying he was ashamed of what he had done, but he was now a changed man. He loved stories of the war and particular regiments such as 'The Gloucesters.' His eyes used to well up with pride and his voice would get louder. He used to sit by his heater in the winter, listening to the radio and writing cards to friends, his pen slightly shaking in his frail yet nimble fingers. Even in hospital, he was thinking of others, particularly the nurses and their families, rather than himself. He told me how the nurses would tell him they had never met anyone quite like him, who would consider others in the ward more deserving of care than himself. One of them had remarked that he was truly a rare soul. He was. I helped him with such simple things, I felt that I barely made a difference, but he said to me once, "You, Simon, are a gift from the Lord." I nearly choked on my tears. On another occasion, he told me how he had been worrying about a situation that he could do nothing about. *"I asked the Lord, and He said, "Tell Simon."'* (I got used to tears.) A simple thing like failing to catch his own fall on a chair, saw him being whisked to hospital, and whilst there, the cancer was revealed. I visited him one morning to check in on him; he was bewildered, confused and thirsty. He lasted a few more days before passing away during the night. Here was a simple man, who unlike many of the others I came across, was more secure in his identity, and secure in his hope of life eternal. He was a friend of Jesus'. I include him in this book as for some reason, for an elderly man I saw just once a week, he has influenced me more than almost everyone else I have written about. I think of him almost daily.

Dear reader, it's time for a change of mood. I can feel a song coming on....

Chapter Nine

Face the music

'I'm trying to find where my place is, I'm looking for my own oasis; So close I can taste this, the fear that love alone erases...

So I'm back to the basics, I figure it's time I face this, Time to take my own advice; Love alone is worth the fight...'

(Switchfoot, 'Love alone is worth the fight', 2014)

A couple of years ago, I was on a family holiday in Cornwall. We had taken the electric car down when I noticed how low the charge was, and how it needed to be replenished quickly, or we would face breakdown miles from anywhere. I preserved the miles by driving slowly enough to a *Nissan* dealer on a country road between towns and sat for about three hours whilst it charged up. As I drank free proper coffee in a china cup and saucer while eating complimentary biscuits, feeling like a free-loader, I turned to a men's magazine and read a feature on *DJ Avicii*. This young man, in the prime of his life and at the top of his music-making profession felt a pressure so great, that he could not hold onto life any longer. It was a story immersed in sadness. He felt alone despite his fame, great wealth and popularity and he only gave a few close people the clues that he was starting to break apart at the seams. The article went on to describe how many musicians suffer from depression, anxiety and suicidal thoughts. It is a massive problem.

Musicians, mental health, depression and suicide

The suicide of Tim Bergling, better known as DJ Avicii, hit the international news on the 20th April 2018. He joined a long list of renowned musicians of whom I have picked out some as pertinent to me for the unifying reasons of having killed themselves (mainly by hanging), because of either depression or depression and alcohol, usually both...

Keith Flint, The Prodigy: 2019- depression.

Chester Bennington, Linkin Park: 2017- depression, linked with alcohol.

Chris Cornell, Soundgarden: 2017- depression and Ativan/Lorezapam (anxiety)

Craig Gill, Inspiral Carpets: 2016- depression, sleep deprivation and anxiety.

Paul Hester, Crowded House: 2005- depression.

Jon Lee, Feeder: 2002- depression.

Stuart Adamson, Big Country: 2001- alcohol and depression.

Michael Hutchence, INXS: 1997- depression, alcohol, cocaine, prescription drugs.

These men had worldly success, but in common with many men in their forties and fifties, they couldn't reconcile something and saw taking their own lives as the way out. There are many more and some had more celebrated names of course.

"He had everything..."

To the casual onlooker as well as the fans, the obvious question comes- 'He had *everything*- why did he do it?' Tim Bergling specialised in EDM-(Electronic Dance Music) and grew in popularity from small beginnings in the Swedish capital Stockholm, to hitting the world stage with the release of *'Levels'* in 2011. His booking fees rose from around $250,000 U.S. per show to around $750,000 U.S. per show in 2012, whilst his annual earnings were reported to be about $15,000,000 U.S. He used painkillers apparently such as the highly addictive *Perocet* and *Suboxone*, as he suffered with alcohol addiction and mental health issues. He was an introvert who also was a humanitarian yet was surrounded by people who may have had no apparent interest in protecting him. Here was a man whom on paper had the world's attention, adored by many, whose music touched millions of people, but inside was anxious and in turmoil as he couldn't make sense of life's meaning, according to his family. The bottom line is that there is a massive problem with mental health decline in the music industry. Much is demanded and therefore the pressure is more than many artists can bear, once established in the public eye.

Can success work against you?

Is it me or does this simply go back to what is common to men (famous or not); hope and loss of hope? I thought about this and about drummers especially, as we are often left in the shadows of the front men and guitarists. I looked at high profile band musicians and I came up with Stuart Cable (original *Stereophonics* drummer), Jon Lee (original *Feeder* sticks-man), Craig Gill (*Inspiral Carpets tub-thumper*) and Paul Hester (*Crowded House founder member*), among others. It was hard to read without feeling deeply-saddened by the stories of their decisions from which there would be no return, and the devastating fall-out for their families. How is that fame, adulation, record sales and careers based on doing something you *love*, could actually work *against* you? Could it be that the reality did not match the outward appearance? You can see how multiple interviews, live shows mixed with lots of travel, recording and hype might be followed by returning home to silence and a slump in mental outlook, just trying to process the madness. It happened to Johnny Cash, didn't it?

Scrabble

For rock and pop stars, I remind myself that they are experts in 'performance mode', and probably yearn for normality in many ways. I remember reading many years ago that the then-household name Robbie Williams was not only hounded everywhere, even having to call time on an *Alpha course* he was taking, but during a documentary in 2002 (*Nobody Someday)* he admitted how he was openly fed up of his life and bored of the songs he would sing nightly to tens of thousands of clamouring followers. He had more rapport and camaraderie while on European tours with his crew members, playing Scrabble back at the hotels, drinking tea.

Maybe there's something in this: the dichotomy of craving worldly success, fame and fortune, yet still wanting to be 'the boy next door' with a normal life of taking the dogs for a walk in the park or having a cup of tea with your grandmother. In my own band days, we were working to a point where we were poised for industry attention, yet I thoroughly enjoyed my job in a restaurant with its simplicity at the other end of the scale. When I worked in the airlines, I felt a similar parallel; on the one hand I could be cruising globally in a position that was craved by so many girls and boys, yet I recognised it was just a job and I often yearned to be back at home doing something normal like fix my bike, play chase-games with my kids or strum my guitar on the sofa. I have grown to love Scrabble and jigsaws too.

The downside to fame

Freddie Mercury was interviewed before he passed away and revealed that deep down, he was lonely and felt unloveable. George Michael felt his life was a 'waste of time', having fallen into a deep depression when his mother died of cancer and his soulmate died of AIDS. The boy bands like Boyzone, Westlife, and One Direction all experienced the hollow times. Just because they sold millions of records, were hounded by girls and boys and adored, doesn't mean they didn't experience pain, isolation and depression. Various members opened up to share that they all did and thankfully showed their egos were not too great to suppress their feelings.

Prince died in 2016, aged 57, from an accidental overdose of *Fentanyl*, apparently a powerful synthetic opioid, many times more potent than heroin. It was revealed that he had to take painkiller *Vicodin* for his hands, or he would not be able to perform and somehow the painkiller was laced with *Fentanyl*. It is also reported that he was depressed and enjoyed sleeping more than anything in his last days. Justin Bieber, Kendrick Lamar, Kid Cudi and Bruce Springsteen have thankfully been vocal about depression and suicidal thoughts, helping raise awareness of this so that other men might feel it's OK to admit they feel the same. There are a myriad more musicians in underground rock and metal bands drawing attention to this problem of mental health instability among musicians in the public eye. It would seem that the more removed you are from the banal everyday acts, the more rarified the atmosphere becomes, and the more vulnerable you become to those voices that lure you into dark caverns which twist on and on and lower below the ground, only just lit by a faint red glow ahead.

What are artists most afraid of?

Financial Instability. Well I guess it comes with the territory. Music is closely linked to fashion (as I tell my own drum pupils). Those beats you hear that are so compelling, so well produced and so energetic are usually recycled every 10 to 20 years. You can be in vogue for a while, but here's the clincher. Music styles in the mainstream often come and go with fashion, and with it, the money. If you persist in sticking to a style or a sound, you are either well-advised or simply bull-headed. Like the acting profession, musicians often sacrifice everything like a normal career, a family or relationships to concentrate on their professional goals full-on. We have all heard the expression 'penniless musician'. While some musicians crave relevance, others demand artistic respect (the avant-garde), and many others still desire simple wealth to display as a sign of their worth to others. We all know how money talks, and how money comes and goes.

Criticism. When you put yourself out there as a poet, a singer, a painter or a photographer, you make yourself vulnerable, exposed to ridicule and open to criticism. Not everyone will like what you produce, as we all have our tastes and preferences. Kevin Carter, the celebrated wartime photographer committed suicide, in July 1994, just 3 months after winning The Pullitzer Prize for an image he took during an African famine, to highlight the suffering there. The photograph of a Sudanese girl crumpled from exhaustion and dying while a vulture waited a few metres behind for her to expire became world-renown. He felt connected to the event and was criticised for doing nothing to help. The guilt inevitably consumed him and pushed him over the edge. Irrelevance. Poor reviews. Failure. You can see how it doesn't take much to fall into poor mental health....

Relevance. Again I'll refer to an up and coming band from Dublin. When asked why he thought they had survived as a group for four decades, the singer-come-humanitarian-influencer responded: "Don't be crap." He added, "Don't embarrass your audience." I'm sure he muttered something too about being relevant to the times. It wouldn't be too clever for any of us to be labelled irrelevant. Mind you, who gave anyone the right to call anyone else that?

The dark side

It is known that the higher up the ladder you climb, and the more you achieve in terms of fame, the more untouchable you are made and the more outspoken you become. You become vulnerable to 'handlers', those who *'made'* you. *'If you want to really make it, you have to do this....'* Forgive me, but I have to ask a painful question, simply because others have asked it too and the answers have not been clear. *What if there was foul play involved in any of the 'suicides' of the most famous, and why?* I have heard of links to renowned politicians. Already I can feel people groaning, however as you will sense, the world can be a deceptive place. As I've written in the previous chapter about 'illusions', so it is with fame. It's not all it's cracked up to be.

Heroes are just as messed up

A good friend of mine (Bobby) and I got to play with one of our heroes doing a solo gig in a small music venue about 15 years ago. When I say 'hero', this guy had played in his own right as a member of an eighties band who had recorded half a dozen albums, did *MTV* and worldwide tours, had gold records on the walls and shared stages with household names and legends of the music biz. Another friend of mine in London had put us in touch. The experience was very different to what I had hoped for. Prior to playing together we had conversed by phone a couple of times and it looked like we might be playing some prestigious festivals too. We shared stories about gigging over the years, but it became clear all was not 100%. From nowhere, mid-conversation he slammed me down. My friend in London explained: "Those mood swings are because he's an alcoholic. He's had other people to do everything done for him throughout his life, and now he's on his own." (Years later, I would work with alcoholics and would understand why.) Here was a guy who flipped from being genteel and immensely likeable to downright aggressive, naming you incapable and untalented to your face. On the night, he decided at side-stage two minutes before show-time that he would do the gig alone, and that he wanted us to stick around as he might call us on. I was incensed. All the work we had put into just securing this gig, all the rehearsal and time spent learning the songs had come to *jack*. I was all for pulling the gear off stage and bailing out there and then, but Bobby convinced me we should wait. Funny what happened next: he played his guitar and sang to polite clapping, but it was hardly earth-shattering, as he acted like a diva on stage berating the pleasant-enough sound engineer over the mic. (I apologised later to the sound-man who smiled and said that he had seen big egos in small venues like this before, and he knew how to deal with them.) After about eight pieces, he announced that he was going to call some friends onstage to play along. I think he sensed it was needing something he couldn't give alone. As I passed behind him, he whispered, "What's your names again?" (He couldn't even remember *that*.) The three of us played one chilled out song with him, to louder applause and then Bobby and I got up to leave. He urged us to stay as he must have realised three were better than one on this occasion as the audience response was livelier. We played a few more tunes together, packed up quickly while our guitar hero was enjoying talking to fans and we never spoke again. Our man was to drive home drunk. A four-hour journey. He dropped me an email to apologise for his behaviour and regarding our playing abilities said we could fit into any professional band, no problem. I don't think I ever replied. Some things just ain't worth it. He turned out to be just another guy who had his moments of fame, but he was just as broken as anyone else. Brokenness can hit any man. It has no regard for your wallet, your circumstances, your fame or your outlook. He did have an amazing guitar collection though....

Glastonbury Farm

A couple of years previously, my band had just come off stage at The Cheese and Grain, Frome. (Well, it wasn't actually the stage, it was a cordoned-off area of the hall as we were an unsigned band with smaller audiences.) A certain lady had just seen us play and was so enraptured by our performance and our singer that she couldn't believe we weren't famous. She told us we simply had to play at Glastonbury Festival, and she would try to pull some strings. That lady turned out to be Michael Eavis' cousin. She managed to get him to agree to see us at another local gig we played in our hometown which turned out to be a near-riot and one of the best gigs I'd ever played. (Unfortunately he couldn't make it as he had to go to a local residents' meeting to discuss the future of the festival. Sometimes things don't happen for a reason.) Following this, I decided to make the call to the organisers and phoned 'Worthy Farm' myself. This was how the conversation went...(bear with me it was a long time ago.)

I spoke to 'John' who sounded a bit 'slow' as he promised to put me through to the office. Eavis himself answered me, in his unmistakeable tone. I explained it was John who put me through, and he sounded confused...

"You said it was John? What's he doing answering the phone? Oh, bloody 'ell no! John?! E's supposed to be out milkin'!!"

Suffice to say we never played Glasters. I wondered if I was ever to fail at being a rock'n'roll drummer, I could probably fall back on a milking career with John.

My last story...

Looking down at the tracks

It was January 9th and the mood in the band bus was jovial. Eight of us were piled in, with all the gear at the back and as we passed Heathrow airport enroute to London, several of us had clocked a sign saying; 'Wild boar'. This caused us to erupt into a famous *Duran Duran* song changing the lyrics to fit. Then a minute later, the blizzards arrived in the early evening skies, just as the weatherman had predicted. Our laughter ceased. The windscreen wipers were going overtime, and the snows were thick. The realisation came as we drove towards Kentish Town, that no-one in their right mind would be venturing out tonight, least of all to go and see a band. It was too dangerous. Even the van skidded on ice near the venue as I attempted to park up on a hill. It was to be an expensive rehearsal, playing in front of just nine people. The managers for two huge alternative rock bands were scheduled to come to see us play but they were of course no-shows. (Management deals: so close, yet so far.) About half an hour before we played, Bobby and I had sneaked off for a burger. We found a bridge with a high wall which overlooked the train tracks below, a complex system of rails, covered in a blanket of white, as we exhaled cold mist against the bright night sky. I remember gazing out at apartment blocks, being mesmerized by the contrast of the black rails like winding needles in the snow. I drove the van home that night arriving home finally at 04.00. I remember staring at the motorway, fighting sleep as the van ate the miles, thinking to myself that this was another point in a sequence of disappointments in trying to make it as a band.

All that way for nothing. Another London gig playing a tiny venue just to get your band noticed. Was this all a waste of time? Nearly killing yourself and others in bad weather. Where was my life heading?

I still remember that icy night, like it was a personal crossroads. There were only a handful of trains that went past below, and I followed their red lanterns as they disappeared into the night ahead along those thin tracks, grinding and rattling into the distance. But it was the tracks which I can't quite forget, almost as if they were symbolic, each one leading to a different destination, a different pathway, a different journey. Three months later we would be disbanded, and I would be taking a different path into the unknown once more.

Chapter Ten

Fight or Flight

When a change in your life hits you, expected or not, you usually have the choice of response. Reinvention is one of those choices when things don't go to plan. (That's if you had a plan in the first place.) Here are some latecomers to the story, but it's just to show you that when life doesn't happen in the way you expected it to go, there are usually avenues you can take or responses you can make. (Some of them may or may not involve animals, chocolate or aircraft.) But it doesn't always mean there won't be any scars left behind....

Thirty seconds to impact: a total Speedbird

In my former book, I described my first long-haul flight for the national carrier, as the lead cabin crew member, feeling unsure of myself and in a surreal situation. On that day, the captain looked strangely familiar as I met him outside the briefing room, and it clicked within forty minutes who he was. He had been the hero captain who had gone against the pilot's textbook by streamlining the wing profile for landing, to gain an extra 50 feet so as to fly clear of a London airport tube station and make it to the runway before the aircraft dropped out of the sky. There had been zero fatalities and he was hailed as a hero with his first officer and the cabin crew who had evacuated everyone safely. And here he was in front of me three years later, in his *Raybans* chatting about it all from the left-hand seat as the 777 smoothly flew the director to Las Vegas, his Senior first officer choosing to sport blue-lensed *Oakleys* instead. Continuing his story, he told me that once back at work a few months after the incident at *Cranebank* the training HQ, other pilots would often sit away from him as he had his lunch in the canteen. He was effectively ostracised by his company, the CEO and colleagues, to the point of being ousted. He had taken voluntary redundancy, expectant of being able to find another piloting job fairly easily. He told me as soon as one particular rival airline realised he was 'the crash-captain', the interviewers made their excuses. His private life was heading for a disaster of its own kind. His stress levels were through the roof and he felt isolated. (Man, this is hard to write, it feels like a newspaper story but let me carry on.) Responding to adversity, his wife more or less became his agent/ manager and they co-wrote a book, 'Thirty Seconds to Impact' which explained the context of that day, and he found himself with a new side-hustle as a sought-after keynote and motivational speaker. He got his old job back too. As Pete talked, turning around occasionally to handle radio messages from ATC centres, I felt truly this was a demonstration of *fight for flight*. This man was a total Speedbird.

Aero to Yorkie

My mate Randy did well. He was a buggy-driver at Gatwick who became a flight attendant for one of the airlines I worked at. We were training course buddies and became friends. We drifted apart to pursue different headings, and lost contact for maybe twenty years. In that time he started a family and became a commercial pilot. When the bottom of the airline industry fell out in 2020, having been furloughed and recently losing his pilot job altogether, he became a delivery driver to bring in the pennies. Realising that this was unsustainable, he very recently re-trained as an HGV driver to boost his income. Now he's a trucker, with a certificate to prove it and only one minor bump down a narrow road against his record. Best of all, he can now rest his right arm on the door frame as he drives, gaining a *trucker's tan*, hoot pretty girls (and boys if he feels like it) and legitimately eat one Yorkie bar per hour. Apparently it's not for girls. He's also a great artist, drawing sketches of classic cars and aircraft. He loves sausages and beans but knows this could be his downfall. He's a complete trucker nowadays and although he may not sit at the controls of an Aero-plane for a while, he's thinking of getting a CB radio. What a ham.

What a shock: don't judge by appearances...

My friend Jammer is a male nurse. He won't admit it, but I think he only did it for the upside-down (fob) watch. (In fact that's the main reason I went for a paediatric nursing degree too but bailed out for childcare reasons.) He's brilliant with car mechanics, the fixing of original Minis and Rileys especially, and his overalls are always filthy. He's an expert at oil sump changes, chassis-welding and all sorts of engine repairs. I think he belongs in 1971. He once managed to catch my dad's boot on fire when he was welding the metal nearby and he also broke my sliding sunroof mechanism one day. I chased him around the car with a ring spanner. It was a very cold night's drive back on the motorway from seeing Lenny Kravitz at Wembley Arena that night with an open roof. (I think I'll retract 'expert'.)

One day, he went to get his exhaust replaced at the friendly car-repairs company who promise you they'll be *Kwik*. Having sorted his pipe, and espying Jammer's nurse uniform, the devious young lad stated the following: "I hope you don't mind sir, but when we had the car up on the ramp I noticed that the shock absorbers were in a bad state, almost dangerous. Now, a gentleman in your line of work needs to be safe, so I'd recommend them being replaced straight away, sir...."

Jammer's reply was a blinder. "That's funny, because those shocks are brand new. I fitted them myself last weekend."

The shamed mechanic muttered an apology and couldn't look at him in the eye. If Jammer was anything like Randy, he should have bitten into a bar of Yorkie, never taking his own eyes off the lad. While taking his pulse with his fob watch.

Faggots and Koi Carp

Following a six-week 'adventure' to the Dominican Republic to assist in an orphanage rebuild, I needed work pretty sharpish on return to the UK, so I signed up to a driving agency and a friend lined me up a day a week at a local butchery run by Mark. Every Tuesday I would make about 400 faggots from scratch, using fat netting, scraps of old meat which I would put through the mincer and then roll them into balls. (Mark couldn't understand why I would always go vegetarian at lunchtimes.) One day, he asked me if I could look after his pet fish supplies store adjoining the butchers. One of my tasks was to change the water in the Koi Carp tank. Mark returned after 30 minutes to find me with a red face, water sprayed over the ceiling, boxes, till and in fact everywhere. He shook his head laughing when I explained that I couldn't remember the correct sequence of turning off hose, pumps and taps. What I wisely kept to myself is that due to my drainage expertise, his prize ornamental *nishikigoi* were seconds away from running out of air as they had been swimming sideways in the last inch of water to get air into their gills, until I found the correct tap and opened it up to their frenzied delight. He never asked me again to look after the shop, as filleting and filtration are not a good mix. You might say I felt like a fish out of water myself. As surely as the sun rises in the east, my days of faggots came to an eventual end in the west.

Change of scene

I know sergeants who have retired from the police force after decades of public service. They have become delivery drivers, gardeners, and charity workers.

I knew a captain on Embraer regional jets many years ago, who had previously been a bank manager. He left the airline, moved to Greece and became an olive farmer.

A drummer friend of mine who used to be in a signed touring band we played alongside, is still a musician but has been running his own business as a landscape gardener for the past 25 years. We got talking about trees vs housing developments and I told him how I often think of him when I'm considering them. Here's what he replied: "Wonderful trees. Given half a chance I'd spend my life in the woods." I told him that he had just conjured up an image, and that was the last time I spoke to him. His band used to be quite poplar. (Ahem.)

Pre-departure one early morning at LHR, we were awaiting passengers to board the A320 to MAN so had time for a quick chat. The First Officer joined in when I showed one of my band's videos on my phone in the galley and said that his old band had been signed to *Island Records* (famous Reggae record label and U2's stable). There was only one other rock band I could think of and yes, he happened to be the old bass player. Of all the local bands in the world, I had their records at home, literally wore the T-shirt (had two of them) and seen his group twice as they were one of my faves, 20 years earlier. I had even nearly joined his new band when the old one split. From emerging rock star to airline pilot, he had lost his hair in the meantime and wasn't quite so slim, but he had played Wembley Arena alongside The Cult. Not many could say that. What a Trouper.

In Lebanon about eighteen years ago I met another flyer, this time a former USAF F1-11 bomber-pilot who had become a missionary. He was more intent on talking about my drumming style, whereas I was wowed by the fact he was an F1-11 pilot.

An old friend of mine worked as an apprentice for Rolls Royce on aircraft propulsion, became a firefighter a couple of years later and then an airline pilot after finishing with the fire brigade. (I called him *Captain Custard*.) Funnily enough, like F1-11 pilot above, I think he ended up becoming a missionary too.

Sorry, it's another pilot. Having worked as a Boeing 737-800 training captain, he left that world of corporate charter flying to set up as director of an M&E (mechanical and electrical) company. He's done some great work for me in the housing development sector. He's pretty much guaranteed *not* to be a missionary, but I'm hopeful....

I know of men who have left the military to become authors and businesspeople. The structure and the discipline of the army, navy and air force lends itself naturally to those prepared to use tactics and strategies to succeed. (You'll always be able to spot a military guy out of uniform. They'll frown visibly at the cost of a beer, as they had it good at the NAAFI and the Officer's mess all those years.)

Then of course, there are men who have 'adapted' in different ways.

Returning home from another London gig in the band bus around 00.30 on a Saturday night, as we were headed out of the capital on the ring road, ahead of us was a man in a pink tutu carrying a wand. As we sailed past, we hooted, and everyone laughed out loud like a bunch of football hooligans. The guy never changed his expression but held his wand as we drove on. I pondered as I drove with my Red Bull in hand. *Why would a stocky man be dressed as a fairy on a roundabout?* It came to me soon after, a country bumpkin who lived far from the bright lights. I felt naïve and sad that someone would turn a trick like that.

Many years back, the restaurant I had worked in was more like a bunch of friends whom you couldn't stop laughing with, than a workplace. Two guys who knew each other through one of my colleagues, ended up doing some part-time washing-up shifts. They were both happy-go-lucky characters who liked beers and dope. I found out that one had been caught stealing from petty cash to feed a more compulsive habit and was fired. A couple of years later, I saw him begging on the streets, and I did a double take from afar. He had no energy and his eyes were bloodshot. Months passed and someone told me he had died.

Fast forward to about a year ago, and I saw another man who seemed familiar in a split-second, shouting to others down one of the city's main streets. It was the other guy, still faintly handsome with shirt open and smiling, but he looked like he may have been sleeping rough. Years earlier, he used to sit in the bar after work, with a lager in hand entertaining us with his dreams of going to Australia and starting a new life in the sun. That dream would be too hard to fight for. Daily, he would finish work and drink until closing time. This carried on for years. He was never even to leave the city. Imagine if instead he had saved £20 a week for a year towards a flight. Vision versus reality. His dream had been broken and himself with it.

Abuse: The world caves in, then rebuilds...

More recently, I felt the need to call a friend of mine, as it had been a few months since we had last talked. (I have learned to obey those tiny prompts that often tap insistently away in my mind, as they nearly always occur at a vital point in time.) I remember standing outside my offices in the car park as we spoke, feeling heartbroken for this gentle soul who was suffering a major breakdown because of evil which had been inflicted on him in the past. He revealed to me through tears, that as a child he had been abused by a trusted family member and the past had now caught up with him to try to finally destroy him. He was starting to have open breakdowns everywhere, even at work, and had been given time off for medical assessments. He felt lost, depressed, fearful and abandoned. No hope, just blackness all around. His world had caved in. Now the guilt and shame had pushed him into a corner as an adult, and he opened up to tell me that he had recently gone to the funeral of a friend who had taken his own life, and was now thinking to himself, *"Maybe that's not such a bad thing...maybe I should go the same way..."* Thankfully, it didn't take much persuading to lead him away from the seductive lie that whispers, *'the world doesn't need you...no-one needs you...this is easier...you won't feel the pain of living anymore...'*

As I listened, I suggested a battleplan, signposting him first to his GP whose influence ought to be able to put some things in place for him to start the protection and healing process. I thought of everything I could to get him started, unsure if my advice would hit the mark. It made things easier to remind my friend that he was an exceptional human being; I really mean that. I remember the first time we had met, and he truly *shone.* He had a warm humanity and an inspiring glow about him. Even if he had lost that spark and the darkness was enveloping him, it would only be momentarily. So ironic that the guilt and the shame are felt by the *victim*, and not the perpetrator. I would keep in contact every few weeks if I could and left him to find himself once again with the help of others.

Present day: I *Facetimed* my friend last week, and was greeted by a smiling, happy-looking guy talking to me from somewhere tropical with the effervescence that I knew well. Light years away from the almost-defeated shell of a man who had only just enough energy to cry out for some help. He was now steadfast on his journey to wholeheartedness and triumph. He is reinventing himself with a new side-career. The gates of hell did not prevail, and he was now no longer a captive to the past. I wish there were more men like him who cut back at the darkness with their inner light, inflicting fatal wounds on demons who cry out in anguish as they have failed to reclaim another lost soul. Their shrieks will be louder now as he helps others who going through the same pain.

When the darkness comes, we men have a choice to make: Captivity or freedom?

Childhood trauma

Childhood trauma is real and can't be buried without it rearing its unexpected head anywhere down the line. No accomplishments, achievements, nor letters after your name can stop the sudden invasion of this monster from wanting to destroy you from the inside, even decades later and without warning. I know of someone else who had been a successful businessman, but now had slid into a series of dark panic attacks over many months that had completely changed his personality, as though he was on the edge of a precipice facing the threat of a fall. No sleep, no joy and no reprieve. So he went to a counsellor and they traced it back to one key thing. Ready? *Undealt-with childhood trauma. The trauma he went through from his father.* It takes you back to childhood and experiencing the fear that you thought had gone forever. That ancient serpent had only been coiled, hibernating, slyly waiting for a moment to seize its prey from within and destroy it by playing back a series of images from the past to remind the victim that it was bound by the past and could never truly escape. He's getting better, as he fights it I'm happy to say, but it's still up and down.

A Saturday-share

About twelve years ago, I enrolled myself on a part-time counselling course at a local college, as I found the subject deeply interesting. One Saturday on an all-day session, the tutor turned to the subject of childhood trauma and explained (paraphrased), "very often it can come from an event such as a car accident, a fall or an abuse which the victim locks away and is then unaware of...until a trigger point like a memory acts as the key which then opens up that Pandora's Box and all the world's evils fly out..." At that point, I had a flashback to something which had happened to me a few years earlier. I had been cycling through town and was just turning onto a high street at speed, when I glanced to my left and saw a blue car driving up a road. In the space of the next couple of seconds, I was acting out my revenge in the most extreme way on a school bully, beating him into a bruised and bloody mess, before pulling him behind me with a rope around his neck, leading him to a high wall on the school premises, near where he had thumped me in the guts one day smiling as he had approached me, a 13 year old boy. *Where did that come from?!* I quickly came to my senses still cycling, thinking my day-dream of the ultimate revenge had come from nowhere, but it hadn't. I had obviously stored memories of his bullying deep inside and hadn't ever thought of them again and didn't even remember them as being of any consequence. I had seen a trigger point twenty years later, and the box was now open. That key, that trigger was the blue car; a Mazda 323 turning up the hill towards my old school. It was that seventeen-year-old bully's car. Perhaps needlessly, I shared my story as an illustration with the group of mainly females. I could see both nodding and worry. Over the next few minutes, I sensed chairs being shifted away from me.

I have already shared a couple of real-life up to date stories of abuse and how it has affected two men I know fairly well. I know that there must be many more men out there who have been abused. The main type of abuse amongst men and women is physical (including domestic violence), followed by psychological abuse, financial abuse and sexual abuse. Do men *really* get abused in any of these ways? Of course.

One of my friends I see once in every few years these days, but we still manage to keep in fairly sporadic contact. He got married a while back and it all seemed to be going fine, until her stress and anger appeared, and my friend began to normalise it. He told me on one occasion his hair was pulled, forcing him to the floor. He has been punched and pushed around, as well as shouted at repeatedly. He's called it *'bad control of frontal lobes'*; hers, not his. They're still together and working things out.

It's funny but when you're in a relationship, you'll do anything you can to make it work, and in doing so perhaps not exactly stand up for what you entirely want, for fear of upsetting the other person and risk losing them or some sort of stability. Relationships are fragile, but they can also be like rubber; quite malleable and resistant to knocks. Yet within that, it is sometimes possible to be oblivious to controlling behaviours. I speak from long-past experience, where at the time I was told I was never quite good enough, didn't earn enough and that I should be this or that, instead of who I was and what I was doing. Looking back I could see how manipulative, coercive and abusive that period was, even though I brushed it off and minimised it. I had to walk away however painful that was, just to be true to myself. Chapters in the book of your life.

I know I've touched on this in Chapter Eight, but for men (and women), breaking up is one of the most painful things that can ever happen. Whether you've been going out with someone a few weeks, or have been in each other's lives for decades, the level of pain may be different, but these elements are common: Loss, emptiness, despair, disbelief, abandonment, betrayal, anger, fear and simple hurt. Nothing seems to matter. I know couples who I thought were solid, loving and unshakeable, only to find myself bewildered when the news came either in person, or through others, that they had separated. It's that ripple effect that touches so many others. However, if you find yourself in a toxic relationship, it takes courage to address it head on. Fight or flight? Only you will know.

Legal kill

Ok, legal head on. In criminal law, there has to be a *mens rea* (guilty mind) and *actus reus* (guilty act) in place to prove culpability for a crime. Hypothetically, if I intentionally took someone else's life against their will, I would be charged with murder, agreed? If there were other circumstances, such as negligence or an accident, the charge could be 'reduced' to manslaughter by just an *actus reus*. Both crimes come under the term 'homicide'. It is a complex area of law reliant on detailed examination of the facts. As I was always told in my legal studies; *"Apply the law to the facts."* So far, so good. Now, if I don't actually murder the victim, but am a third party, aware of the facts and don't intervene to help the victim, then I could be an accomplice or party to the act, I could be charged at least with omission. A duty of care or of rescue would have to be established in that case.

I have only really in the last year or two comprehended the full enormity of what I am about to deliver. What regular murder and manslaughter law covers is sidelined for other members of society, largely down to our 'convenience culture'. Because of The Abortion Act 1967, legal kills of living, breathing yet undelivered babies are allowed every day. In England and Wales for 2019, the abortion rate stood at just over 207,000 for the year according to official government statistics. That's the recorded ones. Add to this the 'DIY home abortion' figures and the floodgates are open. Since March 2020 to May 2021, over 75,000 women in England and Wales will have undergone a home abortion...

There is plenty written about the shame, guilt and darkness that women feel after undergoing a 'termination', but much less so with men. This is *not in any way* to belittle or reduce the emotions of the mothers at all. It is just to say that I am sure that any man worth his honour should be feeling emotional in some way or another. How do I know this? Because about 25 years ago, three close friends at the time were party to abortions. They said hardly anything about it at all and their faces became very grave and troubled when they individually let it slip. Two out of the three relationships ended soon after. In over two and a half decades, those three guys never mentioned it ever again. But I can tell you one thing. If they ever went for counselling, I bet you it would come to the surface at some stage. So, what did these guys do: fight or flight? I am not passing judgment here. I am criticising the failures in law to protect another's life, as well as highlight the fact that *men who are party to abortion/ termination will feel something.*

Words have power, but you don't have to listen to them...

While I was a fourteen-year-old pupil at that same school, I took music lessons. I had two percussion teachers who were ineffective in my estimation. The first told me to hit quietly and was more interested in talking about his passions: imminent retirement and skiing. (I was fourteen; you don't hit drums quietly as a teenager.) His replacement was less positive. One early session, he lazily stuck a chart in front of me, telling me to play it, and expected me to comprehend the strange dots immediately. When I stumbled, he ripped the sticks from my hand, threw them onto the floor and shouted: *"You'll never make a drummer!"* I was shaken, looking down at the floor not wanting to anger him anymore. I stopped going to his lessons and taught myself, which was a hard process, but I got there after months of perseverance, listening to my favourite artists and working things out. I found out that others had stopped going to his lessons too, and he was to soon lose his role there quite rightly. I'll never forget his words and have always struggled with bearded men as they remind me of aggression. He had no place to teach others with such a bad attitude. The biggest irony of this: I am now a drum teacher myself and have been for years, following my experiences during my band days. Occasionally, I have a beard too, but I don't shout at pupils telling them they're failures, or worse. (Unlike the guy in *Whiplash*.)

What is about words that others choose to speak over us like some sort of curse? It's as if those words create wounds, that if inflicted early enough in our childhood and adolescence, will cause devastation ahead like a time-bomb in our adulthood. The moral of the story? Guard your heart. Not everything you hear will be good for your heart. You'll need a strong filter, an internal strainer and an inner understanding that when you are growing up, not everyone will have your best interests at heart.

Chapter Eleven

Sudden Death

You may have heard it cheerily said, "We come into this world with nothing, and we leave with nothing." Or as David Bowie wrote: *'Ashes to ashes...'* Desperation, loneliness, isolation. I was told that loneliness was the biggest killer of older people...and sometimes the younger too. When you receive 'the call', you will always experience that sinking feeling in your heart that someone else has left this mortal coil, sometimes in tragic circumstances, perhaps without ever having felt love, acceptance or life in all its fullness.

Loss of hope

It doesn't have to be something of magnitude like a sudden disaster to destroy hope. It may happen through an erosion over years, a slow-gas which acts like a coiled python around you, gradually anaesthetising your senses until... I often see it on people I pass locally; their eyes are dead, they are going through the motions, organising children, falling into routines, complaining about things which are of no consequence and watching life go by like a bus. Sometimes I feel like this too, and it's dangerous.

Hope. Such a short word, but so powerful. When Terry Waite (the Archbishop's Special Envoy) was kidnapped along with journalist John McCarthy in Lebanon in the 1980's, hope of finding them alive disappeared. Upon his release, I remember reading extracts from his personal diary in a Sunday magazine. He said he claimed to have faith, but it had been exposed as weak, vain and impotent (or words to that effect.) He came to points whilst locked up by Hezbollah, where he doubted he would ever get released at all. Years passed and hope diminished.

The definition of hope; *'A feeling of expectation and a desire for a particular thing to happen.'*

I hope I get chosen for the football team. I hope I win the lottery this week. I hope to see my grandchildren in the autumn. I hope my chemotherapy works this time.

All legitimate, all personal, all longings of the heart. Hope keeps you going. In May 2018 a study of suicide rates amongst men in Scotland by Glasgow University found that of 728 persons who took their own lives in Scotland during 2016, three quarters of them were male.

Under the bridge

Not the frail beauty of that *Red Hot Chili Peppers* song, but the tragic story of an old school-friend's life as he wandered onto the railway tracks very early one morning to meet with his end. I received the call from my best friend later that same day to sorrowfully announce; *"I'm sorry to say that X is no longer with us..."* I was to feel that numbness and hollow sensation that seems to come only with the report of a death. The ripple effect they talk about was more like ocean waves as I thought instantly about what his family must be going through. I still think of him from time to time and wonder if there was anything at all I might have been able to do to stop it. Whenever I go near that bridge, I feel the strangest pull.

Last year I undertook a suicide awareness course called *Suicide First Aid*. (Mindcanyon's details are in the Forward section of this book.) It struck me that the biggest thing I learnt was that if someone is thinking of doing it and maybe has a plan in place (how, where and when) then you can remind them that this is the biggest one-way decision they will make. Knowing this, it should be possible to wait a little longer to think it through, after all what's it going to hurt, to delay things just a day? This may just be the leverage to rethink and avert it. If only I had taken this course a few years earlier....

A grizzly laid bare

My first death to deal with as a housing professional, was a few weeks into the job. My client was a big bearded man, like *Grizzly Addams*, who lived alone in a neighbouring town. He didn't say too much at all. All I did was regularly pick him up from his ground floor flat, run him to the local shops, wait a few minutes and return with him. I would see if I could gently persuade him to engage in any sort of conversation, but he was a closed book with usually short answers. Unfortunately, he had such a disregard for personal hygiene, that I would have to pre-open the windows in the car and put a polythene sheet over the front seat. I felt bad for saying anything, but having endured it for several weeks, I had to cease being polite and start to be more direct. I said to him one day as gently as I might, that it would be a good idea to have a shower and to buy some new clothes. It astounded me that he asked to do a detour on the way home to pop into *Peacocks*. Whenever I left the flat to depart, he would always say 'thank you' in a high-pitched voice which was at odds with his stature and stare into space. That was the extent of our collaboration. I doubt anyone else got too much out of him either. All I knew about his pastimes, was that he went to town to a social club once or twice a week by bus and would watch DVDs to entertain himself.

I received the call at home from a colleague one afternoon who asked when I last saw him, then informed me in a matter of fact way of what had happened. I sat down on the stairs and listened. The police had bust down the ground floor flat door after some neighbours had alerted them, having not seen him for a few days. He was discovered slumped on a chair, surrounded by empty vodka bottles. I didn't even know he was a drinker. The inevitable conclusion was that he had willfully drunk himself to death in one go. I put down the receiver and sobbed immediately. He was gone and all I could think about was the loss, the emptiness of his last few hours and what took him to that one-way decision.

It was now up to my detective work locally to find any family members; all I had to go on was local knowledge as the housing provider nor the police could help with anything. All that the police could tell me was they had used specialist colleagues to deal with the body; 'the dirty- bodies team'. There were no firm details anywhere of his N.O.K, but on notes he referred to a brother and a sister. It was a young man from the local shop who after some quizzing from me, quickly jumped in my car to show me where he thought his younger brother lived. Ironically, it was a very short walking distance over the road from the flat. Using just a hunch, I had found him.

This was the first time I had ever had to announce a death of a family member; a sibling. As soon as his little brother answered the door, I could see the facial likeness straight away... it was chilling for a second. I asked if I could come in and as I told him, the tears came streaming down his face, as he appeared child-like just like his older brother. Because he was well-ordered I quickly found his sister's details and was able to inform her too. She told me how the family had been close when growing up, but their father had suffered with poor mental health and the brothers had been affected too. (Fathers, take note; we are so influential in our children's lives, never forget that.) I then passed over the reins and the handover to his family. It was my first time dealing with the aftermath of a client's death. Other colleagues were very familiar with the legal processes, and I did what I could for the family members before it was time for me to withdraw. I still had clients needing me in the world of the living. My consuming sadness was that there was a life curtailed, perhaps 30 years too early and all because of loneliness and possibly self-loathing.

What more could I have done to help this man? There must have been something. Did loneliness actually kill him?

Too late

I first met *P*, outside the city centre's Job Centre Plus. (Ironic that he used to manage one.) Here was a stocky man in his early fifties, heavily bearded and resembling a mild-mannered *Hells Angel*, he was indeed a biker. One thing was clear on arrival; this gentleman was shaking badly, and deeply anxious about something. He opened up to me within a few seconds. Everything had just disappeared from his life, and he had endured a nervous breakdown. In the space of a few weeks prior to this, he had lost his job, his relationship had broken down and his wife had left him, his beloved dog had been taken away from him, as had his shotgun just in case... If that wasn't bad enough he had been forced to move out of his area and to a new city where he knew absolutely no-one, and was just starting to acclimatize, when he received the call about Universal credit and a new application process being needed. This would mean at least six weeks with absolutely no income at all. To top this, his elderly parents were both close to death as they were diagnosed with cancer, and his immediate siblings were keeping vital information from him. *P* was in fairness, a nervous wreck. In the time it took me to organise myself and others for a funding application, I made a handful of wellbeing check phone calls. The first few were answered, and he spoke about how hard it was with his mother especially so close to dying and his brother making things impossible for him, but the last handful I made were voicemails to his phone with no returns. I knew he had a lot on so wasn't overly worried. He would have been consumed with going to visit his parents. In that space of time, his mother had died.

It was to be my manager who would confirm what I was starting to suspect already. *P* had *'passed away.'* No other information was given to me at all. I received a call from the organizer of a charitable event that was taking place on Christmas Day, to say he had tried to deliver an invitation through the letterbox but was unsure he had the correct address. I had never heard of a door being boarded up so whatever had taken place behind that door must have been like a horror film. A cloak of sadness enveloped me, and figuratively my heart sank like a stone to the bottom of the river. This man had no-one and nothing. No willing family, no friends, no money and especially no hope. And no one knew. His life would have been unacknowledged by anyone in this world. We were all too late.

Could I have done more? Could I have stopped him? What dark passageway was so compelling a route, that this one-way brutal decision seemed to be the best way out?

Ripples on the water

This morning as I write this, I have just received some very sad news. One of my stepsons phoned my wife from school just 30 minutes after drop-off. A friend in his class, someone he knew very well had made the decision to take her own life in the night. Sixteen years old. The shockwave has hit everyone, from school friends to adults and beyond. I can only imagine the despair of her mum, dad and siblings. I never met her, only her mum and younger brother, but I've found myself weeping many times today. The ripples of such a tragedy aren't gentle. They tremor more like a tidal wave. The ripple effect reaches far longer distances than the city limits. It punctures hearts in other countries and continents as word spreads out. *'Someone that was a friend of someone you know'* becomes personal and the grief captures many in its nets. Sixteen. Your life hasn't even begun properly.

Loss of a son

'ICT Director' and I try to keep in touch with every month or two. He lives a couple of hours away from me and we share a love of music, vintage *Gibson* guitars and motorcycling. He lost his boy couple of years ago. His beautiful boy in his late teens who had not even started to *live.* The circumstances were tragic. It was an overdose of a 'recreational drug'. Sadness is hitting me even as I type this. This should never have happened. I had received the phone call from a mutual friend to inform me, and like any event of importance, you can always remember exactly where you were and what you were doing. It was a Sunday morning and I was standing near the spring in my dad's courtyard. I spoke soon afterwards to my friend. A couple of weeks later we attended the funeral and they released some birds outside the church; a poignant moment and an act of letting go. That year my friend also lost his mother, and asked himself; *"How much more can I take?"* While he is still upbeat and appears on top of everything, I'm sure I've caught a faint bleakness behind his eyes. He sighs if the subject ever comes up. I don't blame him. I would find it hard to face each day without some reminder of what happened. To lose a son is to lose that part of a man that might have taken the best of you into the future to make *his* mark on the world.

"How much more can I take?"

I had a call yesterday evening from one of my good mates who as in common with all my friends, (mainly because of the great idea of a national lockdown,) I just don't see anymore. That has never stopped us communicating though. Get this.... "Si, I don't have long to make this phone call...I've got some bad news...my brother's just died. I have to go back to Cyprus to deal with it, and I only just got back from there last week. I just can't believe what's going on. He died of a heart attack they think... and you can't make this up; on the day we buried my mum in Cyprus, having established she didn't die of Covid but of heart failure, I called my partner to check she was OK, but she was crying. I asked her what was wrong, and she told me her dad had just died (in Africa)! On top of that my sister's boyfriend died last month. I just don't know what's going on! Work has finally agreed to give me the time off to deal with everything. It's all happened at the same time. *How much more can I take, Si?!*"

I listened and expressed my own disbelief, but I told him I had no clever answers. I was grateful for his trust in our friendship to tell me such things yet burdened for him. If you're a true friend, you should feel another's pain. Perhaps selfishly I thought when my turn would be. He was right though. All these deaths happened in an unconscionably short time as if to test how much overloading he could bear.

Wigs; a near death experience

It was about one a.m. as we were returning home from a London gig, on a stretch of the M4 motorway somewhere near Reading. It had been an unusually celebratory evening involving a Lebanese restaurant with ten of us at the table pre-show. Bobby and I were driving Gav's old Volvo estate containing all the band gear, messing about with some wigs as we drove, whilst the others were attempting to race us in Nick's Renault 5 laden with five passengers. Predictably they overheated, and we pulled in ahead of them onto the hard shoulder to wait for the breakdown recovery truck and for the car to cool down. I parked up and left our hazards on, and we wandered up to see them. The five of them were effectively standing in darkness a metre away from the slow lane of the road, as the Renault had not enough battery-life to even get the hazard-lights going.

Whilst we were working chaperoning our friends further up the bank, away from passing traffic, which was surprisingly frequent for the middle of the night on a weekend, someone shouted: *"The Volvo!!"* Whilst our backs had been turned, about twenty metres away the heavy Swedish estate had decided to make a quiet getaway, hoping no-one would notice and roll slowly onto one of the busiest three-lane motorways in the UK. I raced without looking behind me, more in fear of scraping the borrowed car, and by the time I reached it, the lumbering estate had just made it to the fast lane and was about to hit the central reservation with hazards still flashing. I scrambled for the door, jumped in and stopped it, before starting the engine and waiting for a moment to drive it back to the hard shoulder. Bobby, meanwhile, without a hi-viz jacket and at incredible risk, was in the centre of the motorway blocking my lane in those precious fifteen seconds and redirecting approaching vehicles away from the Volvo and into the slower lane. However, all it would have taken is for one vehicle to take over-compensating evasive action and five figures standing in darkness next to the slow lane would have all been fatalities. Reunited and out of immediate danger, we all hugged and waited together until the breakdown truck appeared.

Resuming our journey, Bobby asked me how it happened, and I looked at him sheepishly; one of the wigs had been covering the unused handbrake and I had left the car in neutral. (It was the weird curly blonde one that actually did make you look like a sheep.) We breathed a few thanks before laughing almost until we cried. The events could have been very different indeed. You never know how thin that strand that separates life from death is until you experience it. Ironic that Nick had penned something a year before which the band had recorded but never played live: 'Car Crash Song.'

A personal loss

I received the call on a beautiful June day, while I was on the early shift as duty manager at a private school. I cycled straight to the hospital in 20 minutes flat, feeling light tears behind my shades as I thought to myself; *"Could this be the day that I knew would come...?"* My mother aged 62 had suffered a brain haemorrhage at home. They had been watching morning television, drinking their first strong coffees of the day, when she announced that she didn't feel well. She then laid down on the floor, struggling to breathe. My dad panicked and rang the pharmacy instead of the ambulance service. An hour or so later, when I arrived at the ward, she was being kept breathing by life support machine, eyes closed.

The nurses left my dad and I to have our last private moments with her. The strangest thing happened there; as I walked around the bed, I accidentally knocked it and I saw her covers wobble. In a flash I reverted to a five-year-old boy and as I looked down at her, these words sprang up in my head; *"You're my mummy... I was in your tummy."* I was shocked. *Where did those words come from?!* Within a few minutes, the nurses and the presiding doctor approached us tenderly to say they were going to switch off the machine, so we should be saying our final goodbyes. My dad and I wept together, he in total shock, whilst I switched to autopilot so I might carry us. Outside, I called my sister in Greece and stammered, "She's gone." Ness dropped everything and flew out that night from Santorini. As I stepped out back into the sunshine, a line from a Depeche Mode song came into my mind; *'Summer's day as she passed away...',* but I didn't think God had a sick sense of humour. My mother had probably suffered because of a latent deep vein thrombosis (DVT), which may have taken a while to suddenly explode, taking her from this life into the next. Later that afternoon, when much of the admin by phone was completed, as I sat down in the garden with my dad, I asked him if there was anything he needed.

"Yes...Father Tom is coming at three. Could you buy me some wine from down the road?" 'Sure,' I replied. "How many bottles? One, two?" He paused to think. "Er... no...make it six." That's Catholic priests for you. As it happened, they got through just one bottle together as Father Tom was driving. (Incidentally there was a deal on six. Being an ex-caterer, my dad was never one to pass on a deal.)

Fast forward to my Mum's funeral. As we arrived in Gav's Volvo, I drew up to the burial plot, stopped and turned off the engine. *'This is notta dee place,"* announced my dad quizzically in his strong Italian accent. "What do you mean?" I replied. "They've put that sheet over the mound and the digger's there." My dad once more said the same thing. *"It is notta here, it is further up that way..."* He was right. It turned out to be the first time in the crematorium's 100-year history that they had dug the wrong grave, meaning we had to return to the church hall for the wake, which would allow them a couple of hours to dig the right grave. My mum would have enjoyed that as she did have a wicked sense of humour. With comic genius, Gav sidled up to me, all six foot six inches of him, and with a glint in his eye said to me and a couple of others in a low voice and factual manner; "You know they've got a pet cemetery here...."

I retorted quickly; "What? You want my mum to be buried between a Chihuahua and an Alsatian?!" She would have probably preferred that as an option. It was the Cornish in her.

When your mother goes, you never forget her. Why did I become a little boy once more when she lay motionless? Is there really a special bond between a mother and son? Yes there is. It's called...

Attachment

No, not the Word document you have just finished for the presentation tomorrow. So much has been said about *attachment theory,* that I almost feel patronising of your intelligence to bring it up and even explain it, but I'm going to assume you might want to know a little more, just in case.

It is a complicated subject, and I don't do complicated, so here is a simple take on it, and counsellors can feel free to correct me. It basically sums up the emotional closeness you had as a child, especially with your mother. How loved you felt, how connected you were to her emotionally and how present she was for you in the first couple of years of your life. As I wrote earlier-on, the attachment you had as a child may explain issues of self-worth, abandonment (just like Greek Gangster) and the ability to love and connect with others.

It doesn't stop there; it extends to adulthood and how you relate to your partner. How you were loved as a child has a direct relation towards how you interact as an adult. It's a lot to take in there. I thought I was OK before I knew about attachment theory. Now I can see I have probably been carrying things I knew nothing about for years. Nothing sinister, just things. I realise I was probably a little subservient to my mum, but I did give her a run for her money in my teenage years. I even called her 'a cow' one day. You can imagine how well she took that after raising me for so many years. (I may as well tell you how I came away from that one.) *"What did you say?!!"* she growled. Realising I was cornered, my 16-year-old-self retorted; "Er...there's a cow looking through the window." (It was plausible, as there were fields behind us.) Even my dad had to look away smirking.

I loved my mum really. I hope I've taken the best bits of her, like her laughter, her perseverance and her hope. I think I've inherited her ability to use a paragraph when a couple of words would suffice. She was great at chivvying me up when I got down. She used to love giving me those little inspirational booklets filled with all sorts of encouraging quotes and aspirations. Yes, some could be a bit girly, but I liked that.

Death. We'll all have to deal with it at some point, even if it's simply our own.

I've carried the coffin of my best friend's dad. Afterwards, I cried as it was taken away in the hearse.

In my previous book I described a day when I was called away from a computer terminal and taken to a hotel to deal with a distant-colleague's death. Nothing dark had occurred but I had to personally orchestrate the deceased's removal from the hotel with four others, using blocked-off corridors and a tiny service lift. Five of us stood silent with his black body bag on a low trolley at our feet. I only began to process it several days later when I saw the obituary on the wall at HQ and his face; it was then that it hit me.

I watched my father throw rose petals as his wife's coffin was lowered into the ground, sobbing heavily which set me off. As I shook, the policeman's hand firmly gripped my arm from behind me, as if to say; 'Be strong.' (In case you're wondering, I wasn't in trouble with the law; he was a family friend. But it still felt like an arrest.) We are nearly at the end of this story now, so you might as well see it through....

Epilogue

Mistaken identity

'Who am I? Where am I? Why do I feel this way?' (Jesus Jones: 'Who? Where? Why?'1991)

Man, the provider. Man, the hero. Man, the athlete.

Man, the brave. Man, the lover. Man, the rock. A man for all seasons?

I guess the pressure is on, then. If it seems like too tall an order, then it probably is. If I get my identity from my job, then if my job is taken from me, then my identity has gone with it, and it follows that I am now without identity. This sounds harsh, but I am talking quite literally. If I get my identity from anything temporal, anything or anyone that can be taken from me, then it surely follows that my identity is balancing precariously, like a tent in the middle of a snowstorm pitched on a crevasse up Mount Everest. That would be a mistake.

So, it follows that my identity is something which is *cultivated,* deep within through the storms of my life, the uncertainties, the misfortunes, the low and desperate times and the hardships. Those moments from which I never thought I would rise again and see hope. Just as I would slowly read *The Desiderata* in the quiet illuminated porch of that majestic church, I recall that line about nurturing strength of spirit for the hard times (paraphrased). If during the good times, I didn't make ready an anchor for those hard times, I would be truly lost at sea. I sometimes wonder how thin that line is between holding things together and losing the plot altogether, considering the lives of those gentlemen I helped in my advocacy role. You realise that this is so commonplace. Up and down our beautiful lands, men, women and their families are struggling with debt, finding work, making rent, affording food, coping with illnesses, wayward children, addictions and ASB. Behind more palatial settings, in the grand homes of cities worldwide, you will too encounter loneliness, addictions and even an imitation of life. For those of us who are somewhere in the middle, we are not immune from any of this. Sadly, often all it takes for our world to crumple is loss of employment, a relationship breakdown, a bad review, a public ridicule or simply loss. This balance of mental health though, is something that affects *every single one of us*.

What is that us men really need?

A listening ear and a chance to be heard. Acceptance and not judgement. A beer with a friend who can make you laugh. Sometimes tangible help with worries concerning money, home, jobs and relationships. Every so often, a can of silicone spray or a new set of screwdrivers can really help too. We have basic needs. We are quite simple really. (Women are now nodding their heads in agreement.) In reading this book, I want to thank you for seeing it through to the end. The reason I write primarily, is to reach out and say: *"You are not alone in your brokenness!"* There are more of us men about who secretly, and occasionally openly, feel the same. You may think otherwise, you may think you are unnecessary, have no usefulness to others, or question your worth. Just as Michael Stipe sings so longingly; *"Hold on...hold on...."*, so you and I must.

Why? Because the world needs men who are overcomers, weak yet strong, authentic, brave, passionate, tender, full of laughter, serious when we need to be, willing to lift others, risk ridicule and the taunts of lesser persons to emerge triumphant. If this sounds quasi-medieval then I make no apologies. It really is a war out there and all around us are boys wanting to be shown how to be men. (Look at me. See?) Having seen what has happened to these men I described, to my heroes, to my peers and to people I know personally, my conclusions are heading in this direction...

A broken man's thoughts

What you experience as a child will often shape who you become.

If you don't feel loved as a child, it'll be harder to show love as an adult.

Our children really need us to be present and loving, for it will shape their lives.

Negative words spoken over us are hard to shake off but shake them off you must.

Fathers should not underestimate their influence, for it runs through generations.

If you don't break free from your parents, you'll find it hard to find your own path.

Prisons can be of our own making. Forgiveness, love and acceptance set you free.

Carrying negative baggage throughout your life is unnecessary and destructive.

Talk about your stresses and release them, rather than compressing them inside.

To believe or have a faith in something greater than yourself gives you purpose.

To end your own life is an act of desperation, and widely felt is the ripple effect.

A decision to take your life can always be delayed. A little more time could heal you.

Hope is what you cling onto as the promise of better things to come.

Hope and faith make life worth living; they are described as this....

Jeremiah 29:11 'For I know the plans I have for you, declares the Lord, plans for welfare and not for evil, to give you a future and a hope.'

Hebrews 11:1-2-1-2 'The fundamental fact of existence is that this trust in God, this faith, is the firm foundation under everything that makes life worth living. It's our handle on what we can't see. The act of faith is what distinguished our ancestors, set them above the crowd.'

(The Message)

What solutions are out there?

If you've wondered about it, but put it off for another time, then I can suggest a couple of things I have undergone which have really helped me to process and to move forward. If the old ways don't work, then try something new...

Counselling. It really helps. The counsellor helps me to explore me and what I have experienced, to process and find new direction. Costs about £50/hour in the UK.

Coaching. All of the ideas come from me, and as it's progressed, I have realised that it's only been me who has been stopping myself. Costs vary, but similar to the above.

Quiet time. For me it has been with my Maker, aka 'JC'. Other people call it meditation. It takes the focus off me and onto the One who has the bigger perspective. Plus, it's free. (Or maybe He just hasn't billed me yet).

Laundry. I was asked recently what things I do to improve my own MH. Yes, I hang out my family's washing. There's method in my madness, as it gets me out in the fresh air, away from the laptop and free with my thoughts. Costs about £2/ full load, covering electricity, water, detergent, fabric conditioner and soda crystals. Benefits? Immeasurable. I think I'm going to start a campaign: *Real men do laundry.*

Why I write

When I look back at some of the things which have happened to me, I think my pathway could be used as both a warning and an encouragement to others. The title 'Journey...' came to me in a whisper, making sense instantly. He only gave me that one word. My wife in comic mood finished the rest of the title. (I think I even found it funny too.) Even if this book speaks to just one and encourages him, then this has all been worth it. The last thing I wanted these pages to be is an 'advice-book' so please take it as an experiential offering to you. There are many experts out there with far greater worldly credentials than myself, but I reckon as we are all so unique, perhaps I had to share my own stories. As I maintain, I am no expert, but I have had enough varied experiences to tell this tale, so here they are. Sometimes experts have all the theories but lack the stories. That's where I come in....

If you want to contact me, you'll find a way. Call me old-fashioned but I like letters. (I also like stickers, especially surfing or skateboarding ones. When I was younger, I was often told I looked like a surfer; it was my wild hair. I once accidentally managed to surf over my wife's head. That's why I stick to body-boarding.)

So, as I say goodbye (and parting is such sweet sorrow), may your own journey fulfil everything you were ever born to be. Keep going. *Seriously, keep going.* Don't give up. Your life is too precious beyond words to have it stolen from you.

I've said enough on this occasion and it's time for me to go quiet. Always watch the quiet ones.

THE END (maybe...)

P.S. You may wish to check out Dr. Gabor Maté: this gentleman has revolutionised what I previously understood about addictions, diagnoses, stress, illnesses, attachment and treatments. I would signpost you to investigate his findings. They turn everything we think we knew on its head.

With thanks to -

Drum Teachers
07808003372

622 Teachers Listed 03rd Jun 2021

Printed in Great Britain
by Amazon